The ABC's of Enneagram Types

Learn how to improve your friendly and loving relationships. Understanding who you are, growing spiritually and finding your inner path has never been easier.

Marion White

© **Copyright 2024 Marion White - All rights reserved.**

The content contained within this book may not be reproduced, duplicated or transmitted without direct written permission from the author or the publisher.

Under no circumstances will any blame or legal responsibility be held against the publisher, or author, for any damages, reparation, or monetary loss due to the information contained within this book. Either directly or indirectly.

Legal Notice: This book is copyright protected. This book is only for personal use. You cannot amend, distribute, sell, use, quote or paraphrase any part, or the content within this book, without the consent of the author or publisher.

Disclaimer Notice: Please note the information contained within this document is for educational and entertainment purposes only. All effort has been executed to present accurate, up to date, and reliable, complete information. No warranties of any kind are declared or implied. Readers acknowledge that the author is not engaging in the rendering of legal, financial, medical or professional advice.

Table of Contents

Introduction..6

Chapter 1... 14

What does it mean: "Enneagram Types"?

Chapter 2 35

Type 1: The Perfectionist

Chapter 3 45

Type 2: Selfless / Helper

Chapter 4...64

Type 3: Manager

Chapter 5..**86**

Type 4: Artist

Chapter 6..**101**

Type 5: Observer

Chapter 7..**113**

Type 6: The Collaborator

Chapter 8..**125**

Type 7: The Hedonist

Chapter 9..**137**

Type 8: Leader or Challenger

Chapter 10..**149**

Type 9: Diplomat or Peacemaker

Chapter 11..**158**

Subtypes

Chapter 12..**169**

How to Recognize Your Type

Introduction

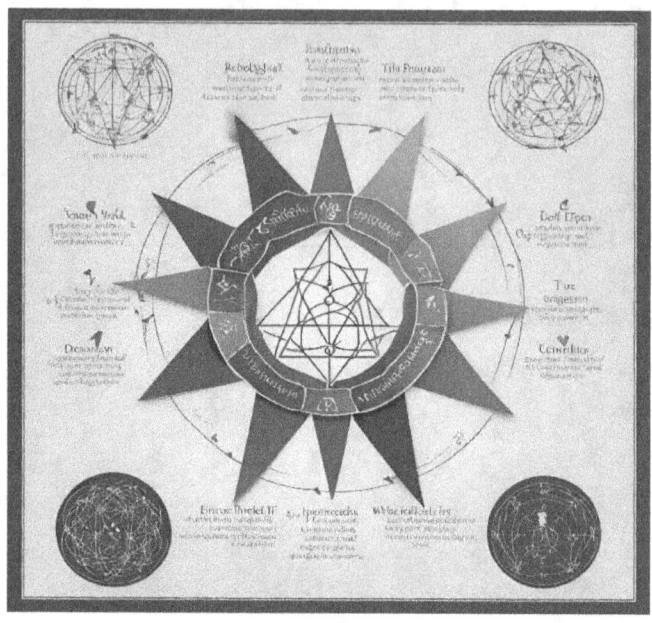

Observe, and ask yourself: what is it that usually fills me with anger? Do I let it out freely, sometimes even exploiting its power to get what I want or do I tend to hide it under a mask made of rigidity? Do I rationalize the situation from a superficial point of view and completely ignore any emotion that is capable of bringing down that wall that I have built with so much pain over the years, disappointment after disappointment? What would I think if I were a stranger watching me in this state? Would I be able to love myself, allow myself to feel emotions and express negative ones, or would I fill myself with guilt, shame and fear?

Let's take a deeper look at the example of anger: imagine, for a moment, finding yourself in those situations in which anger takes possession of your body.

Now hold back this feeling for a while, without judging it and triggering a conflict, observe how you behave, what your thoughts are about it and what lies behind that anger.

Anger

Perhaps you will answer: that other person is unreliable! And blah, blah, blah ... Despite this, what others are doing does not really interest us at this moment, because the information you have is the mere personal interpretation you make of their actions, what leads you to believe that they are acting only to hurt you.

Do you often feel that others just want to hurt you or do you often feel that too much is being demanded of you, that you are being judged unfairly, that you are given too much responsibility, and you, on the other hand, feel helpless and frustrated? What is the inner dialogue you undertake with yourself? The deeper it goes, the more you will be able to dig, and gain clarity and answers. In this state of exploration, you will be able to understand how deep are the roots of the behaviors and habits you have learned. Often, we learn to react in a certain way from childhood, during which, like the children we were, we did not have the skills necessary to make our dreams come true and we needed others to do it for us.

Once we have learned this way of reacting, as well as the basic fear and desire that always lurks behind this anger, it is easier to get out of our prison. Now we are no longer children, we are able to take the reins of the situation, satisfy our own needs, understanding the meaning our emotions have, listening to them deeply, replacing our automatic reactions of all time with conscious decisions, inspired by the intimate and profound knowledge of what is really happening to us. Knowing yourself is, perhaps, the most difficult and also one of the most important tasks that we must undertake. Some signs show us whether we have succeeded to some extent or not.

We can say that no one succeeds entirely, as the process is highly subjective. We are both the subject who knows and the object to be known. This makes it difficult. Accepting and valuing oneself is one of the signs of self-knowledge. Only those who accept and value themselves can live in a satisfactory way. For this reason, self- knowledge is so important, since the way we act and the goals we achieve largely depend on it.

Education and the context in which one grows up, make the process of self-knowledge difficult. Each person is interpreted by those around him, from the moment he is born and in an inevitable way. In other words, others attach meaning to who we are and what we do since we start living. This interpretation is not always, or rather almost never, correct. It has more to do with the others than with ourselves. The process of knowledge, therefore, begins with detaching oneself from these ideas.

How to know if we know each other or not? We immediately list some signs that indicate this.

Seeking Your Truth in External Factors

One of the signs that we don't know ourselves is a tendency to seek answers, reasons, or motives from some external factor. We don't believe there is wisdom in us. We underestimate what is in our soul and, therefore, we validate only what is outside of us. Perhaps we often do not realize that, as far as our feelings, emotions and our lives are concerned, there are no possible answers outside of us. And if there are, they are always partial and possibly erroneous. Nothing and no one have the right to tell us what to do or how we should feel. The answer to all this is always found within us.

Compare yourself to others

Comparing ourselves to others is a wrong way of answering questions about "who we are" and "what we are capable of doing". It's not true that if he can, then we can too, or vice versa. If everyone goes in a certain direction, for example, it doesn't necessarily mean it's the right way. Comparing oneself to others, one falls into a trap. Does it seem reasonable to you to compare yellow with blue? Is it valid to make a comparison between water and land? Confrontation, especially when it is obsessive, only causes frustration or false self- love.

Regretting having said "yes" or "no" is one of the typical signs of a lack of self-knowledge. There is a certain doubt in the face of all the decisions that need to be made. It doesn't matter if it concerns big or small aspects, you always doubt and many times you end up opting for something you didn't really want. We say "yes" or "no" because we feel that a situation or a person is putting pressure on us. We do not consult with our heart or mind or experience before committing ourselves to the answer given and we end up regretting it.

Seeking the approval of power figures. Power figures exert a great fascination on those who do not know themselves. It is an unequivocal sign.

In reality, the quality of these power figures is not evaluated, but their importance is attributed and their approval is sought, regardless of the values they represent. Approval by a power figure compensates for the feeling of uncertainty caused by lack of self-knowledge. It is a way of replacing the bond with one's ego with an external agent with sufficient strength to dilute personal insecurities.

Give great importance to criticism or mockery. Since we have not developed a personal criterion for evaluating our actions, we place excessive value on the opinions of others. If this opinion is positive, there is serenity. If, on the other hand, it is censorship or reproach, the world collapses. Depending on the opinion of others is a sure way to gradually deform the image you have of yourself. Of course, we all want others to accept us and have a positive opinion about us. This, however, cannot be achieved at the cost of sacrificing one's identity, otherwise it turns into slavery. If you make a mistake, you want to die. When we don't know ourselves, we judge ourselves with great severity. To know is to understand and when it is understood, judgments are relativized. Not only are the results observed, but also the processes, causes and consequences. Understanding elicits more benevolent reasoning.

If we make a mistake, we can forgive ourselves more easily, because we understand that it is part of a life lesson. If we don't know ourselves, we face the error as a threat; we are afraid of being annihilated and disappearing.

Reacting impulsively in the face of conflict. Those who know themselves do not feel attracted to conflict. He knows that his emotional energies are limited and that he cannot allow himself the luxury of wasting them on useless exercises. The opposite happens to those who do not know themselves: they seek conflict as a means of reasserting themselves. However, he never seeks major conflicts, but rather trifles. One of the signs that indicate a good degree of self- knowledge is self-control. Those who know themselves know how to manage emotions and rarely let themselves be carried away by an immediate impulse.

Otherwise, the person snaps like a spring even in the face of trivial situations, because he feels that almost everything puts him at risk. Self-knowledge is a lifelong task, but any effort in this sense is useful. And it is because it allows you to reach a greater degree of awareness, independence, freedom and security. Do not deny yourself the opportunity to navigate the puzzles and wonders of the most important person: yourself.

Chapter 1

Types of Enneagram

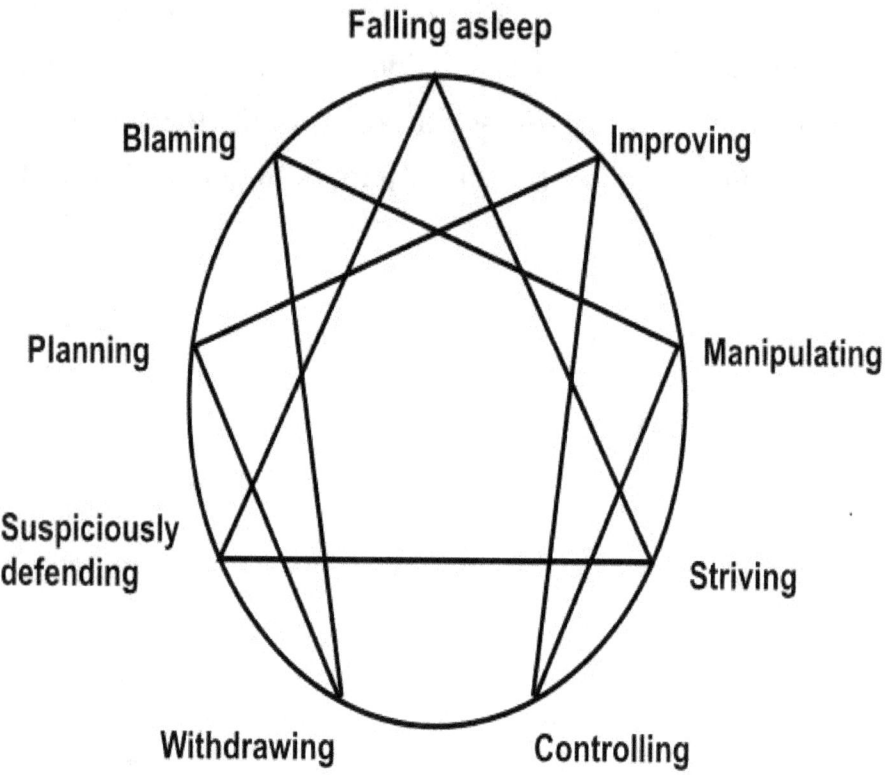

The Enneagram is an ancient method for identifying the type of personality. Enneagram is a word that derives from the Greek in which "ennea" means 9 and "gram" means drawing, therefore "9- point drawing". In fact, the symbol of the enneagram is a 9-pointed star inscribed in a circle that represents the 9 types of personality. This symbolism has been used in various religions and schools of philosophy. It is easy to find a little bit of yourself in each of the 9 types, although one of these should stand out from the others and feel closer to you. This is your personality type.

Beauty captures attention, personality captures the heart. The exact origins of the enneagram are unknown, some trace it back to about 2000 years ago by linking it to ancient, secret Sufi brotherhoods, others to the school of Pythagoras (it is the ninth geometric figure of the Pythagorean figures). In the early 1900s it was introduced to Europe by the Russian Gurdjieff who used it to help his students grow spiritually.

But it was after the 1960s that this instrument began to be studied and spread in the West, when Oscar Ichazo and Claudio Naranjo reworked it in order to use it to investigate personality and character. The enneagram is a personal growth tool that can be used to develop a deeper understanding of yourself and others.

What are the types? Already in childhood it can be seen if a child exhibits one type rather than another. Many of the leading experts in the enneagram are convinced that we are born with a dominant type of personality, supporting the "innatist" hypothesis. Usually by the time a child is 3 years old, the predominant type can be identified. Through interactions with parents, in the first years of life at home and the accumulated experiences, the personality type can be established from about 7 years old.

There is no better type than the others as each has their strengths and limitations to overcome. In fact, although an individual remains with his type throughout his life, there is the potential for an evolution that is limited only by time, awareness and the desire to change and improve.

Wings. There are no pure types; each is a unique mix of its basic type and of one or both types adjacent to it in the circumference of the ennagram. Wings are the "second side" of your personality and must be taken into consideration to understand yourself or others more deeply. For example, a type 9 may have a wing in 1; this means that it will also have some type 1 characteristics. The neighbors to your base archetype could be your wings.

Perfectionist.

He is motivated by the need to live his life in the right way, following his moral principles, including improving himself and the world around him. He fights for his great ideals. Strengths: idealistic, ethical, honest, productive, possesses a high self-control. Weaknesses: critical of himself and others, judge, inflexible. As children they were empowered enough to assume a role almost like a parent, they focused on meeting the expectations of parents and teachers by refraining from doing things that would not have been approved.

They have a very active internal critic that tells them what they should or shouldn't do. They are constantly looking for perfection and think they always know what should be done and how. They are very mental people in fact they are often out of touch with their feelings, including the anger they express as irritation, resentment, indignation and guilt. It is as if there are two selves: a controlled self that cannot let go and a secret self that would like to do what the people it condemns do.

Selfless.

Motivated by the need to be loved and appreciated by others, he is constantly seeking approval and social status. People and relationships have a high priority for twos. Twos tend to be kind, empathetic, caring and responsible.

Strengths: sensitive, generous, flexible, caring.

Weaknesses: victim syndrome, manipulative, possessive, hysterical. As children they were very sensitive to criticism and disapproval and tried to please their parents by being loving and cooperative. Often when they grow up they will look for a profession that leads them to work with people, especially in the role of helper (teachers, nurses, therapists).

They are primarily concerned with helping others in order to be loved, a kind of self-centered generosity. In fact, the approval of others represents the confirmation of their value, which is why they tend to become the people who think others would like them to be and may suffer from low self-esteem.

Manager.

He is motivated by the need to achieve success, be productive and avoid failure. He is self-confident, results-oriented, has excellent organizational and planning skills.

Strengths: self-confident, efficient, practical, energetic, organized

Weaknesses: narcissistic, superficial, vengeful, highly competitive, conceited

As children they were given attention and were rewarded when they got results. Their performances were valued more than their involvement with people. Often as adults they take up professions in the managerial field or where they can occupy leadership positions (IT, legal, financial fields). The three most oriented towards Type 2 can become teachers or salespeople. Winning and being number one is very important to them, they are very competitive, oriented to achieve success and achieve their goals. The threes often expect to be loved and appreciated for what they do and for the results they achieve rather than their uniqueness. They often confuse their true self with their job.

Artist.

He is motivated by the need to express his feelings and to be understood, he is looking for a meaning in life and he wants to avoid an ordinary life.

Strengths: empathic, artistic, introspective, intuitive, creative

Weaknesses: depressed, moralistic, fickle, stubborn, introverted and reserved

They were children with a strong imagination, often organizing creative and original games even in solitude. They are very sensitive and often think they are not suitable or not understood; when they feel not understood they can become rebellious or anti-authoritarian. As adults they often take up professions such as therapists, teachers or related to the world of art. They have a strong inclination towards creativity, art and the romantic. They are sensitive, melancholy, very emotional and tend to dramatize their emotions, in fact they tend to depression. They are often lonely souls in search of beauty and with a desire to be loved and feel unique and special. They tend to find themselves better in one-on-one relationships than in groups and can be very helpful with those who suffer.

Observer.

He is motivated by the need to know everything, to be independent and to avoid looking silly.

Strengths: curious, analytical, sensitive, wise, objective, intuitive

Weaknesses: intellectually arrogant, distant, critical of others, insecure

As children they often spent a lot of time alone reading and preferred a few special friends over large groups. The 5s do not like to work with others and often undertake scientific professions or in some intellectual field. Those who have a 4-strong wing can become musicians, consultants or writers.

They are very curious and brilliant, they have an independent mind that asks many questions, they always have a personal point of view on the situations that they analyze in detail and with a critical spirit. 5s may have a hard time making something happen in the world (procrastination) and often have poor social skills. Also, under stress they can have uncontrolled outbursts of anger.

Collaborator.

He is motivated by the need for security. They are friendly, nice, trustworthy, sincere. They are very concerned about any threats; they are very conscientious and can become paranoid.

Strengths: Responsible, reliable, devoted to family, friends and causes.

Weaknesses: insecure, always on the alert, judgmental, rigid, on the defensive

Although the "six" can be found in different professions, they are often attracted to those in the field of justice and / or academic paths.

He is looking for security both in work and in relationships. In friendships they are very faithful and loyal and tend to prefer long- term relationships. The "six" have difficulty coping with anxiety, suffer from various fears and have difficulty trusting because they would be exposed to attacks and therefore vulnerable.

Hedonist.

He is motivated by a desire to feel pleasure and plans enjoyable activities to contribute positively to the world. They are narcissists, rebels, dreamers, and often deny that they have any problems, especially those of an emotional nature.

Strengths: energetic, exuberant, spontaneous, optimistic, enthusiastic, self-confident

Weaknesses: narcissistic, impulsive, possessive, self-destructive, superficial

As children they were adventurous and in search of exciting stimuli; they are "socialites" and prefer to be in company rather than in solitude. They often change jobs, avoid any repetitive and monotonous work, preferring one that always gives new stimuli and challenges (for example, pilots, photographers...)

They are often remembered for their words rather than their deeds, making great planners looking for future possibilities. They tend to seek new and different stimuli, they tend to do many things at the same time, exploring different things but without going into depth.

Negative feelings cannot be tolerated and they have an attitude of not taking life too seriously in order to mask the deepest emotions. They have many relationships and often change jobs.

Chief.

He is motivated by the need to be independent and strong and to avoid feelings of weakness or dependence.

Strengths: independent, protective, self-confidence, assertive, loyal

Weaknesses: despotic, aggressive, skeptical, self-centered, insensitive

They often had a difficult childhood, dominated by stronger people who wanted to control their life. They learned that the only way to get respect was by hiding their weaknesses and showing themselves strong; for this they have developed a strong independence and a fighting spirit.

The "8" are attracted to professions where they can demonstrate their ability to take on responsible roles and their ability to solve problems.

8s are leaders, fairness and power are important values to them, they are protective with friends and family and are very loyal to those they trust. They have a poor tolerance for frustration and can become inflamed with anger quickly. They are intuitive thinkers and give "gut" responses.

Diplomat.

9s are motivated by the desire to maintain peace and harmony, connect with others and avoid conflicts. The nines have many variations in their personalities, from polite to slightly rude to independent and convincing.

Strengths: available, generous, seeks union with others, open-minded, empathetic

Weaknesses: insecure, distant, stubborn, apathetic, judgmental

As children, they could feel ignored and think that their wishes, opinions and feelings were not important. They are good listeners, objective and excellent mediators. They often work in helping professions and are very supportive of their family members and friends.

The dream of the ideal meeting and union with their beloved is extremely important for them; they can be very possessive and jealous. The 9 have difficulty making decisions and establishing priorities, avoid conflicts and sweep problems under the rug, for these reasons they can be procrastinators and have difficulty managing anxiety.

The three triads (or centers)

Triad. Within the enneagram there are 3 triads or centers of 3 types, that share certain similarities. There are three types in the feeling center, three in the thought center and three in the instinct center. Each center therefore contains 3 personality types that have in common the strengths and weaknesses of that center.

The triad of the heart (center of feelings) - Types 2-3-4

The types of this triad tend to be particularly in touch with their emotional sphere, with their internal image and focus a lot on the relationships they have with other people and with themselves.

The head triad (thought center) - Types 5-6-7

Those belonging to this triad have very intense mental activity and often identify with it. They tend to respond to situations with fear and protect themselves by moving away from personal and intimate involvements.

The belly triad (center of instincts) - Types 8-9-1

Those who belong to this triad tend to act impulsively and instinctively, they are particularly in contact with their physical body and the typical defense mode is attack.

Remembering the impossibility of enclosing the multiple facets of a person in a single category, the Enneagram is an excellent tool to increase awareness about yourself and other people, to recognize and amplify your strengths and intervene in your aspects. A distinction that few makes is that this system is not used to "put you" in a category but to understand which category to "leave" to enrich your personality.

So, what is the use of studying the enneagram?

It mainly serves to understand ourselves, to understand what is the nature that moves us, the way we see others and the world around us, what are our expectations, our way of reacting to external interference, the reason for our emotions and feelings, constructs and values, behaviors and choices and decisions we make (feel, think, do). Having made this discovery, the second in order of time, but not of importance, is to no longer judge ourselves and others for our / their behavior: we begin to see the "game" that everyone plays.

A game that when it reaches the top of the trip makes you smile lovingly and compassionately, especially if the other has the same character as you. I mention, for example, something that happened to me when I went to university. I had to prepare for one of the most difficult exams: construction science. To trust each other we started studying in twos. My colleague was delighted because, having worked as a surveyor, I am ahead of her (statistics has always been my only advantage over high school students). In fact it seems to me that I am more of one who gives repetitions instead of one who studies together with another.

Let's go to the written test. I do the task and pass it on to others too, and we pass it in the percentage of 78%. Let's go to the oral. My study colleague passes it; not me! They ask for the mathematical proofs of the formulas for the calculation of structures.

I am appalled as Analysis 1 was a first-year exam! Then you cannot learn a structure by heart... especially those that we architects invent: if you understand the fundamentals you can understand what will happen and you can explain what you have to calculate, how and why the structure does not collapse ... the formulas are already written in the manuals and if you know which ones to use, you don't need to know how to prove them mathematically. It is the first problem ever in my school life!

Never failed, never postponed, never missed a shot!

A misstep in the most difficult exam to pass. I knew of students who had retired because of that Prof. (a bastard engineer!). I'm destroyed! Devastated! I have feelings of total desolation; I think I have no chance to recover. I lock myself in my sister's trailer for a whole afternoon.

Total darkness. I can't even cry. I feel like I'm a zombie. At a certain point something clicks: "Listen: that moron of a prof., he fucked me up asking me some totally out of place questions! He did wrong, not me. I'm right! And just to show him in two months, I come back without studying anything, except the formulas by heart, twenty minutes the day before the oral.

If that's what he wants, he'll get it; but I show him that he is incompetent and I the magician, the cool one, the one who will go down in history. I proceed like this: I go back to the next session; the writing is more difficult than the first time. I pass it but I learn it on the day of the oral exam because since I am sure I have passed it; I go directly to the faculty on the day set for the oral exam without asking the secretary first. The percentage of the promoted fell to less than 5%.

A few seconds before sitting down for the oral exam, I tell the students present that I have studied the mathematical proof of the formulas by heart, in just twenty minutes the day before, and that now they will see the miracle that proves that this prof. does not understand a thing!

I sit down, unfortunately with the assistant ... I was hoping to find the Prof. Everything goes to God ... after the usual demonstrations go to serious questions. There I give my best. It seems that we are there with 30/30.

The assistant opens the booklet and sees that two months before the prof gave me a nice "RETIRED" for the same exam. Be thrilled! He asks me what all this means. I see the Prof. partly looking at us. He has listened to me!

Great! It is the moment!

I challenge their way of doing exams to a great extent by saying that I have only memorized what they wanted but that, in working practice, it will be absolutely useless! I know that I am taking risks.

In fact, I get 27/30. I get up, say thank you and leave the classroom like a hero, amidst the astonished and incredulous looks of the students who attended the exam. I go home and I perceive that the whole universe is waiting for nothing but my joy to expand everywhere. Boys, this is a pure character 2!

Let's try to analyze the story.

"In fact, it seems to me that I am more one who gives repetitions instead of one who studies together with another."
"I do the task and I pass it on to others too."

This is what happens to character 2 when, in order to be seen as the top of the class, he pretends to be the Red Cross nurse on duty. His gratuitous generosity hides the need to be accepted as the top of the class. By doing so, in many situations, he eventually tends to find himself easily suffocated by his own commitments.

"You can find the formulas already written in the manuals and if you know which ones to use, you don't need to know how to prove them mathematically ".

He immediately reaches 80% of the knowledge needed in a given discipline, showing himself so good at billions of things, even very different from each other. The last 20% is often missing, which usually represents the state of the art.

"I'm destroyed! Devastated! I have feelings of total desolation; I think I have no chance to recover. I lock myself in my sister's trailer for a whole afternoon. Total darkness. I can't even cry. I feel like I'm a zombie. "No one will ever see character 2 in the abyss of the deepest pain! Maybe my wife saw it. For other than when he falls into that unhealthy place, for him there remains little (a few hours).

A cool guy can't ruin his image. Never.

"At some point something clicks". It's nature! Life itself is a miracle and character 2 is here in this universe (it is not known if it is the only one) to demonstrate it. How do you prove it? With a beautiful miracle, with something that no one can ever do again.

"A few seconds before sitting down for the oral exam, I tell the students present that I have studied the mathematical proof of the formulas by heart, in just twenty minutes the day before, and that now they will see the miracle that proves that this prof. doesn't understand a thing! " Jesus never said before what he would do with water, with Lazarus, with the man born blind ... character 2 instead announces itself! It's the only flaw, but after all, you need certainty that the world knows.

"He asks me what all this means. I see the Prof. partly looking at us. He has listened! Great! It is the moment!" From the outside it might appear like the one who finally has the courage to say what he thinks, a fair one ... Character 2, on the other hand, is destroying the opponent, annihilating him with such strong conviction, with such confidence that nothing can stop him.

"I get up, say thank you and leave the classroom like a hero among the astonished and incredulous looks of the students who attended the exam. I go home and I perceive that the whole universe is waiting for nothing but my joy to expand everywhere". Every 2s dream! The miracle has come true once again. Getting to know each other allows a Counselor not to confuse his nature with that of the client while the latter talks to him about his life.

A character 2 after a while would tend to talk about itself to the customer, for example.

The enneagram allows you to cleanse yourself of these behaviors through the study of virtues, but the discussion of this topic would be really too long. Suffice it to say that if studied with that purpose, the enneagram allows you to do a nice personal job because it is based on real life, in the relationship with oneself and with others.

Chapter 2

The Perfectionist Ennea Type 1

The perfectionist is that type of personality that tries to improve things, since it considers that nothing is perfect enough and therefore there is room for improvement in everything. They are idealists who strive to put the chaos in order and are very attentive to detail. They are always attentive to their own mistakes and those of others. They need to improve everything and this can be good in some cases but counterproductive in others. The inability to achieve perfection, in Enneatype 1, makes him feel guilty for not being up to some situations and also fuels his anger at imperfections in general.

Anger is usually expressed in the form of impatience, frustration, annoyance, criticism, and judgment. Although this Enneatype is generally good-hearted, the anger it builds up can lead to occasional attacks. Those with the strongest characteristics can also be intractable, while the "healthiest" ones can be loyal, responsible and very capable friends. They are people of strong and sound principles who follow the rules, unfortunately they expect others to do the same. They are generally practical, well organized, hardworking, honest and respectful people. They are more practice- oriented, organized, honest and respectful but their ongoing commitment to improve and attention to detail continuously makes it difficult for them to relax. They always put duty before pleasure. Emotionally they tend to be repressed and it is very difficult for them to express feelings of sweetness. They typically see emotionality as a sign of weakness and lack of control. On some occasions, due to perfectionism, Enneatype 1 can be confused with Enneatype 5 which, however, unlike type 1 which tends to anger, tends instead to worry and anxiety.

Key Trends:

They want to be right (according to their parameters). They continually strive to improve everything, to be consistent with their ideals and to be able to justify themselves and their conduct. They try to put themselves in the position of not being criticized by anyone.

When it's healthier:

Reliable and responsible, he likes to keep traditions and things that are done right. He takes the job very seriously and fulfills his duties. Respects agreements. He radiates confidence and is available to help others.

Lost quality:

The ability to be in a good mood, laugh, and do fun activities (things he should learn from Enneatype 7 instead).

Fixation:

Perfectionism. Nothing is perfect enough; it can be improved.

Breaking point:

Embittered character, people disappoint him over and over again.

What to avoid:

Avoid the tendency towards Enneatype 4, in which case Enneatype 1 would be seized by continuous bad moods and irrationality.

Characteristics of the Enneatype 1

If perfection exists why not seek it, perfection is possible. He believes that people lack the will to change.

They believe they deserve no love if they are imperfect. They rationalize anger to justify it.

Rigid and critical.

They always try to correct others and sometimes it may not seem like they do.

Hardly spontaneous and have a hard time letting go of pleasant things.

They believe they are always right. They grew up quickly, they didn't play. They rarely lose their temper.

Morally unassailable.

It is the character furthest from spontaneity.

They perfectly control what and how they express themselves.

Ability to always find the "error".

They feel good, superior and this gives them the right to ... We do not accept trying to change continuously.

It is correct or....

They express the aggressive component through criticism. He has a lot of pent-up anger.

They may seem aristocratic in their behavior.

Obsessed with order, cleanliness and how they place objects.

It is very difficult for him to expose himself too much because it means going outside the "norms".

They are very responsible and inflexible. They control their impulses.

Very similar to English high society (Lord behavior).

Reformers, they believe they are doing things for your own good (they actually want you to be like them).

They manage to be great inquisitors and then feel frustration. Pleasure is not part of his goals.

They are generally cold and serious.

Good citizens and very respectable people. Loyal, fair, faithful and energetic people.

People who take life very seriously.

Sober.

They get very angry to the point that they are sick.

When they believe that they are not loved they suffer a lot, because they have worked hard to be loved.

They are puritans, when they impose a rule, they follow it to the maximum. (Neurotic component.)

Enneatype 1: Lead a consistent and error-free life

Anyone who has seen or read To Kill a Mockingbird will remember one of the most beautiful characters in the history of literature: Atticus Finch. His profile, his will, his high humanity and his balance perfectly symbolize the brightest and most developed Enneatype 1, with no areas of error or dark sides to work on. His vital energy and his sense of justice are the characteristics par excellence of this enneatype. Before reaching this level, Enneatype

1 tends to move through convulsive seas, due to complex contradictions and high levels of frustration in which its aspirations are not always realized. Let's see below what characteristics it usually presents taking as reference the description offered by Claudio Naranjo in Character and Neurosis:

Obsession for details. Lists for just about anything, as well as patterns, reminders, etc.

Every task has to be perfect. However, this need is at the same time a source of constant frustration because they never feel satisfied. This behavior leads them to exhaustion, often involving others in this effort, to the point of creating tensions and disagreements.

They are conscientious, often inflexible, and scrupulous.

They have a high sense of justice, of what is right and wrong (according to them), of what is desirable and correct. In their inner dialogue there are many "shoulds", and "musts".

They don't usually delegate tasks to other people, hardly team up or trust others in business matters because they doubt, they can be as effective as they are.

They are very attached to their things, their possessions, their family... an often-unhealthy attachment.

A detail that Claudio Naranjo emphasizes about Enneatype 1 is that it usually has an emotional background inhabited by anger. This dimension gives its character rigidity and a lack of spontaneity. This anger is merely the result of accumulated frustration and the feeling that there is an excess of injustice, neglect, or bad deeds around it that are beyond his control.

How can Enneatype 1 achieve personal fulfillment?

When people of Enneatype 1 work properly on problem areas such as repressed anger, the need for control or extreme perfectionism, they can become profiles with high discernment, wisdom and good judgment. They can become authentic Atticus Finch able to inspire others, guide and influence in an enriching way.

But how to do it? By becoming aware of their attitudes or areas of error. Let's see how.

By reducing their exaggerated idealism.

Lowering the volume of that critical, sometimes even hypocritical, inner voice that requires a moral virtuosity that sometimes not even they can achieve.

Reduce the "shoulds" and self-impositions that often make prisoners, surrounded by very limiting demands.

Learn to delegate, trust others a little more.

Understanding that the world, people and many things around us cannot always be what we want. Living is above all "being and letting be", and it means allowing others to act as they want without this depriving us of peace and calm, without fueling our anger and giving us further frustration.

Make contact with your emotions and channel them, release them.

All this repressed anger must dissolve, any dissatisfaction must find better ventilated areas in which to understand that perfectionism goes hand in hand with usury, that iron discipline leads to exhaustion.

A healthy and exhaustive Enneatype 1 is above all a person free from their mental attachments. In this noble aspiration to reach a more just world and a higher and perfect being, there is an intermediate sphere in which one can feel truly fulfilled and useful.

It is a psychological layer in which emotions are more adapted and where there is a humbler acceptance of reality. When you stop being an internal and external "error chaser", you start living with calmer and satisfaction, being more flexible and compassionate.

Chapter 3

Selfless / Helper Type 2

They are people who have a good image of themselves. Love is their highest ideal. For them love can do anything and for love everything is worth it. They are warm and emotional people who care a lot about their personal relationships, devote an enormous amount of energy to it, and hope to be appreciated for their efforts.

They usually participate in society with a social conscience and are outgoing. They are the kind of people who remember everyone's birthday and go above and beyond to help out a colleague, spouse or friend. They are people who usually thrive in the helping professions. They are tactful with people; they perceive them emotionally. For them it is very important to be able to help others: it is a gesture that makes them feel good about themselves and above all important.

Enneatype 2 individuals are convinced of their disinterest, and it is true that they are often genuinely available and concerned for others. It is also true, however, that these people need to feel needed. But the love they give is not entirely without reason; they give to receive. Ennatype 2 tend to develop a sense of entitlement when dealing with people closest to them. Because they have sacrificed themselves for others, they begin to feel indebted to them. They can become pushy and demanding if their often- unacknowledged emotional needs are not met.

They can be manipulative and try to command others: they feel fully justified in doing so as they "have earned the right" and their intentions are good. The darker side of Enneatype 2 appears when they begin to feel that they will never receive the love they deserve for all their efforts. Under such circumstances, they can become hysterical and irrational. Because they tend to help others to meet their needs, they can forget to take care of themselves. This can lead to physical wear and tear and emotional exhaustion. Enneatype 2 need to learn that they can only be of real help to others if they are healthy, balanced and focused on themselves. These individuals feel bad about themselves if they don't play an obvious role in helping someone in their life.

KEY REASONS:

They want to be loved and they want to be needed for others, to make others respond in front of them.

WHEN IT'S HEALTHIER:

He knows how to give warmth and support, he likes to help and comfort those who suffer, he likes that others need him and he is happy to make himself available to others. He likes to laugh and see others happy. He really appreciates that there is affection in relationships and puts love into what he does.

WHEN IT IS LESS HEALTHY:

Lost quality: The ability to contact one's needs, recognize them and ask for help

Fixing: the overabundance

"I have so much to give ...", "I need ..." Passion: pride

Because he does everything with good intentions, he ignores criticism and does not recognize his shortcomings. When cheerful enneatype 2 tends towards enneatype 8, they become aggressive and dominant.

Characteristics of the enneatype 2

I think: they only see me if I am wonderful.

They have a form of superiority over good and evil They are free, spontaneous, sensual

There is no need to compete, they already feel the best

They praise and are generous but to confirm that they are

They can be very capricious and explorers of the other Manipulators

If they don't have one, they make sure to find a reason to feel needed

They need to feel needed and wanted

He neglects his own needs in order not to know his true self or essence

They believe it is a privilege that others relate to them Freedom is very important to them

They have very chaotic minds The defects are not seen They have a lot of confidence

They usually have a seductive father and an overprotective They fall in love and quickly find out when something is

I'm above the rules and the good and the bad They ask for a lot and don't give much

They are very theatrical, very manipulative of hysteria They are more inclined to action than to think

They are sure to please

Fixation: life is beautiful (false abundance) They overestimate love, emotion

They have the idea that everything is loving, always justified

"I praise you because you praise me"

They promise more than they give, they think they give more

than they give and that is their problem Neurotic Patterns of Enneatype 2 PASSION: Pride

The "pride" of Enneatype 2 can be understood as an imaginary exaltation of its value and attractive power. These are people who have a good image of themselves. They tend to be considered "more gifted" than others. They deny many of their own needs by trying to "help" others.

FIXING: Overabundance

It is the rationalization of pride. It is the thought by which they support their sense of greatness.

DESIRE: Feeling loved

The need to feel special of Enneatype 2 is satisfied by the love of the other. It is the other who confirms his inflated sense of his own worth. The fact that this confirmation is achieved with love corresponds to the childhood frustration they suffered.

DISTORTION OF DESIRE:

The desire to be loved degenerates into the need to be needed.

SELF-IMAGE: I help

They see themselves as people who help others. Helping others makes them feel great. But this help is selective, only for those who consider it. Behind this "helping" a neurotic "giving in order to receive" can be hidden.

FEAR: Feeling of need

Because of his self-image of self-magnification and generosity in helping others, he fears that he too has needs (emotional and affective needs); this could indicate that he is not great.

His greatest fear is that of being unworthy of love and of alienating his friends and loved ones.

WAY OF MANIPULATING THE OTHER:

By discovering the needs and wants of others, thus creating addictions.

JUSTIFICATION: helpful

He explains his actions as gestures of altruism.

WAY OF BEING AGGRESSIVE TO THE OTHER:

Enneatype 2 individuals, fearing that they are neither wanted nor loved, make others feel unworthy to give love, generosity, or attention.

DEFENSE MECHANISM: Repression

The term "repression" refers to the mechanism that prevents certain internal urges or desires from becoming known. By responding to these impulses, but without cognitively recognizing them, one can have an attitude of irresponsibility and give an impression of falsehood.

NEUROTIC FEATURES:

WISHES TO BE SPECIAL and feel better than others. NEED FOR LOVE, delicate feeling. He needs erotic love.

Tenderness and possessiveness.

SEDUCTION, effort to be warm, attractive. He seduces those he perceives as people of value.

ASSERTIVE, dominate, subdue. Strongmomentum and disinhibition.

HEDONISM, pleasure-oriented character. Difficulty in the face of pain, conflict and frustration.

HISTRIONISM, makes scenes to get attention or get away with it. It does not accept rules or limits. Susceptible.

OPPORTUNIST, gives to receive, helps to feel important. He gets angry if his wishes are not met.

Enneatype 2 ideas

CRAZY IDEAS:

Because I am special and better than others, I deserve love and appreciation.

I always have a lot of love to give.

Love is the most important thing in this life.

If you want me, you have to desire me, satisfy my whims and guess what I want.

Those who contradict or judge me don't want me.

I seduce and like myself because I am very attractive.

I don't need the other, but he needs me. I need to feel needed.

I have to be important to be happy because I deserve it.

I have to be independent, better that others depend on me.

If someone loves me, I must be the most important thing to him / her and must always be available for me.

The pain is unbearable, it can annihilate me, it is better to seek pleasure.

HEALTHY IDEAS:

It's best to accept and acknowledge your limitations. I don't have to try so hard to look special to be loved.

Frustration and pain are part of life, things cannot always happen according to my wishes. I can accept the pain and the pleasure.

I don't need to try so hard to seduce and attract everyone. Love is important, but so are wisdom, creativity and other values.

I also have needs; I can ask for help or advice and recognize my shortcomings.

I can devote myself to the experience and accept what life brings me.

I can count on the fact that things flow naturally without having to manipulate reality.

I can accept that some people love me and others don't.

Virtue of Enneatype 2: humility

Humility is recognizing one's own truth and sharing it with others without falling into enlarging one's image, that is, recognizing mistakes and one's ignorance, accepting criticism.

Humility is simplicity, releasing grandeur and understanding that you are one among many.

Let go of the addiction to love and pleasure, accept that pain exists, that things don't always go the way you want. Recognizing shortcomings, what is missing, learning to ask instead of demanding.

Attitudes that improve the Enneatype 2

He must be more aware of the effort he continually makes to please others and must not place much value on how they perceive it. He must remember that it is impossible to please everyone. Furthermore, it is not certain that others will express a possible liking in the way we expect them to, they can do it in a more subtle way or just in a different way. It's important to remember that if you don't feel loved, it doesn't mean that others don't love you.

Be honest with people. Don't systematically compliment and engage in other manipulative behaviors to win people over. Don't make yourself completely available to others. You can help them, but to a certain extent, that is not "all or nothing". Remember that the first person you need to help and care for is you. Do not give too much even in an altruistic way, maybe then you will miss it. Be aware of the real reasons that drive you to help or give to others. Learn to become aware of the process of "giving in order to receive" and / or if there is a search for wanting to feel good as a motive for beneficial actions towards others. You have to be very honest with yourself about your intentions.

Be aware that your pride compensates for an unconscious feeling of not being wanted. A greater dose of pride and arrogance means that the person suffers more that feeling of not being wanted. You don't have to be the best to be loved. Your attitude must be more realistic and therefore humbler, but without falling into false humility, which is also a form of pride. Be aware of your limits, you cannot do "everything". You too are human, flesh and blood, you get tired and need rest. Make sure you stick to your limits.

Subtypes of Enneatype 2 Conservative subtype

Of the three subtypes of Enneatype 2, this is the one where pride is least noticeable and the one that most clearly prefers to receive rather than give. Outwardly it may have an apparently more childlike behavior. It is the most emotional of the three subtypes.

They are called "privileged" for their tendency to consider themselves deserving of special and better treatment ("toast that isn't broken is for me"). More than wanting to be important, they really want to be assisted (I'm the "little princess"). They are capricious. If they are denied what they want, they can get angry.

Like all enneatypes 2 they are great seducers and manipulators, but unlike the other subtypes, they take these attitudes from a more childlike position, in a way more like a child would. The goal of Enneatype 2 in this subtype is to earn the love of others by providing them with the help or assistance they need. They are happy to provide such aids. They are able to anticipate people's needs and try to meet these aids. After taking care of others for a

while, they tend to expect others to do the same for them. "They have the right to "... be treated preferentially." As if they have the belief that by doing the right things, they deserve that life is "right" with them. In this exchange of "help / favors" they may overestimate their action and expect to receive a lot in return.

They can act with superiority towards others and expect preferential treatment that reinforces their pride. It is difficult for them to ask others directly for what they need. They expect them to give it to them without asking (as they are supposed to have done before). Sometimes, instead of asking directly, they drop clues in hopes that the other person will respond by offering them what they need. If the other person doesn't, they can get angry and let off steam easily (childish behavior).

Angry, they may seem like enneatype 8. In the way they expect special treatment, they can sometimes look like enneatype 4. But enneatype 4 tends to seek this special treatment as a compensation for unfair treatment in life.

Instead, Enneatype 2 of this subtype tends to feel that he is "entitled to ..." as a reward for all the things he has done for others ("after all I have done for you"). Enneatype 2, belonging to the conservative subtype, tends to be very protective and attentive to their friends and family, and can sometimes compensate for feelings of loneliness or rejection by indulging in tantrums about material objects, sweets or food. This personality pattern is a little more prone to eating disorders.

They are also more prone than the other subtypes to suffer from melancholy and psychosomatic illness. These disorders can also be a way to seek more attention, express anger indirectly, and hurt those who care about them. When Enneatype 2 individuals are healthier, they are loving, attentive, and generous. They help others without expecting anything in return. There is a balance between their needs and those of others.

When they are less healthy, it is difficult for them to ask for what they need directly. They feel they have a right to have their needs met and expect others to know and give them what they need. They can act in a self-centered and childlike way.

Social subtype

Of the three subtypes of Entype 2, this is the most intellectual, restrained and disciplined. They are the ones who care most about their public image. They are used to being sociable and cheerful (similar to 7-year-olds) and thrive on interactions with their friends. They love to relate to people and are used to creating social networks in which they interact with agility and ease. They know how to sell / seduce / manipulate. Sometimes they can be confused with the social enneatype 3. They can put more energy into the group than into themselves.

Social enneatypes feel loved and occupy an important place in the lives of their friends and family.

They try to attend meetings and social events. They try to make themselves indispensable to the groups they are involved in. They are used to acting as advisors, coordinators and anything that involves the participation and help of others. They can represent the role of the person that everyone needs.

They have good "radar" to catch people who may need their help. Above all, they love to help important people. They are called "ambitious" because they want to stand out in society, they don't want to go unnoticed. They want to do something important in the world and they feel capable of doing it. He has to be someone and he has to be recognized en masse.

They tend to be self-centered. There is some confusion between being loved and being recognized. For this they try to surround themselves with socially recognized people, successful or famous people.

They seek attention both for their efforts and successes for social purposes, and for being close to other people with this social recognition. They are used to taking a leadership position or being alongside the leader, whom they try to seduce.

Sometimes they become "the power behind the power" to relate to and influence powerful people. They could marry someone important and focus their efforts on their spouse's aspirations, such as a "first lady". The ideal they pursue is to be socially recognized by their social welfare actions.

When social enneatypes 2 are in a healthier state they can exert much effort for people and social causes. They strive for the group, but they also take care of themselves. They are excellent organizers of social events and have the ability to deal with people in different fields. When social ennea-types are in a less healthy state, they fear being forgotten by others and try too hard to be recognized and popular. They can put too much energy into trying to be seen with successful or important people. If they feel ignored, they can act defiantly or nasty to get noticed. They focus so much on social relationships that they can put little conscience into their well-being. They can also engage with too many groups or people.

Sexual subtype

Of the three subtypes of Enneatype 2, these are the most seductive and aggressive. They can't stand being rejected, so if they feel like they are, they reject them first.

They are very proud. They are called "conquerors" because they are very seductive and love to do it interpersonally (one by one). They want to win over all the people they care about to "make them theirs". Sexual Enneatype 2 feels loved when it gets close to people. Try to win over or seduce the people they love by focusing intensely on the other's needs, hopes, and interests. It's as if they get in tune with each other.

They enjoy discovering what the other likes, be it a hobby, a music or a restaurant. Then he will do everything possible to provide these things to his loved ones, with the ultimate goal of conquering or seducing them.

They also seduce with praise; they can make the other feel like the recipient of their adoration. They try to be as close to their loved ones as possible. For these individuals, the romantic life is essential. In their intense love life, they tend to confuse being loved with being wanted and therefore they tend to provoke desire in the other; they feed on this desire.

They are used to combining charm with sex appeal. It can be a challenge for them to be able to seduce someone and they can put a lot of energy into that. Sometimes the way to seduce can be aggressive. They may also lose interest in the seduced person and have more interest in those people who have not yet been seduced. They promise more in their relationships than they actually give. When sexual enneatypes 2 are healthier they have the intuitive ability to know the needs and interests of others and know how to get closer to people. They are good at perceiving and interpreting each other's non-verbal language. When the sexual enneatype 2 is less healthy, he is able to do anything to reach the other, especially if there is a love interest. They may fear being rejected and hiding their true needs behind their apparent generosity.

Chapter 4

Manager Type 3

People corresponding to enneatype 3 are characterized by a tendency to seek / need the approval of other people to feel worthy, so they strive to give an image that leads to that approval. Enneatype 3 are generally working, competent, competitive and pragmatic people. They usually know how to make a career out of their great ability to grasp the needs of the environment and want to be admired for their achievements. Consciously and / or unconsciously they tend to try to embody the image of success that is promoted by their culture. They are very focused on finding their goals for which they can be admired, such as being the most successful salesperson in the company or the "sexiest" woman in their social circle.

They can find an area in which to excel and find the external approval they desperately need. But while Enneatype 3 focus their energies on success in any area, they often secretly suffer from the fear of being or becoming "losers". Sometimes, they may have difficulties in the private sphere. Their need to be approved of often hides a deep sense of shame for who they really are and subconsciously they fear being exposed if another gets too close. Enneatype 3 individuals are usually generous and nice, but they are really hard to get to know. When a person of enneatype 3 is less balanced, they can become cold and ruthless with others in the pursuit of their goals.

The problem with Enneatype 3 people is that they confuse what they really want with what the "character" they play wants. If an Enneatype 3 has a "good" job and an "attractive" partner, he may be willing, through an act of self-deception, to ignore the internal impulses that tell him that neither his job nor his partner satisfies his deepest needs. Even the most "successful" enneatype 3, who generally seem very happy, often hide a feeling of dissatisfaction in their depths.

KEY MOTIVES FOR TYPE 3:

They want to be approved of, have attention, be admired, stand out and impress others.

WHEN IT IS HEALTHIER IN TYPE 3:

He knows how to shine with his own light for his personal magnetism and for his ability to pursue goals and reach them effectively. Challenges stimulate him and he doesn't stop in the face of difficulties. They are passionate about things that people appreciate but that only a few can achieve. He knows how to bring people together around a goal and motivate them to fight for it.

WHEN IT IS LESS HEALTHY IN TYPE 3:

Lost quality:

The ability to be anybody and to feel surrounded by loyal and quiet friends (Enneatype 6)

Fixation: deception

"People are guided by appearances" "Everything has to be made up to make it acceptable"

Passion: vanity

He never misses an opportunity to amaze his admirers When the workers of Enneatype 3 tend towards Enneatype 9

they become apathetic and disconnected from themselves.

BEHAVIOR TYPICAL OF ENNEATYPE 3

Glory comes from the approval of others They have an idealized image of themselves

The focus is on being effective and successful Value is put into what it does, not into being He is a compulsive creator

It poses challenges They are controllers

They perceive very well what is expected of them and give it

As children they are very cooperative and brilliant: cheerful, outgoing... but very cold

They know how to sell well, they create their own mask and sell it

Try to be applauded, praised. They weren't very popular children

They are very autonomous because they are successful thanks to a great effort

They are emotionally cold (there is emptiness inward)

They have everything under control: they are "perfect". They wear a mask. They show themselves impeccable and despite this they are not happy

They can generate a lot of success and a lot of money They can come to sell themselves as a product

They seem sincere but they are not They are very insulting in their criticism They are experts in social skills

If they are not successful, they suffer They depend on their apparent image

They make sure that no flaws appear in their external image They have a hard time expressing unscripted emotions

"I make up therefore I exist"

With their successes they feel recognized

The world is a deception, it is a theater. People pretend

"I shouldn't have any problems because if I disturb others and I can't disturb anyone"

There is no acceptance of criticism He needs to feel useful

He can be a beggar but he has to wear a branded suit

NEUROTIC SCHEMES OF THE ENNEATYPE 3

PASSION: Vanity

Vanity is an intense concern of living and distinguishing oneself in the eyes of others, giving more importance to appearances than to one's own experience.

FIXATION: Deception

The vain believe that other people also work on appearances, and therefore it is more important to pretend than to be.

DESIRE: To be admired

They subconsciously believe that when they have done enough to feel worthy and successful, then they will have all the admiration and attention they desire. For Enneatype 3 to be "admired" is akin to being "loved".

DISTORTION OF DESIRE:

The desire to be recognized degenerates into an obsessive pursuit of success.

IMAGE OF ITSELF: The "successful" ego

They tend to believe that they will be appreciated and loved for what they do (and not for who they are) and therefore try to give a successful image. They have a hard time distinguishing what they really are from what they appear to be.

FEAR: Failure

They fear failure because they believe they will be appreciated and loved only for their successes. They are afraid of being despicable or of having no intrinsic value.

WAY OF MANIPULATING THE OTHER:

He looks charming in front of others and adopts any image that "works".

JUSTIFICATION: Efficiency

It is repeated that things must be done "well" and "rightly", but also effectively and efficiently. These people tend to be competitive and strive to be recognized for their achievements.

WAY OF BEING AGGRESSIVE TO THE OTHER:

Enneatype 3, fearing they are useless and worthless, make others feel useless by treating them with arrogance or contempt.

DEFENSE MECHANISM: Identification

Tendency to identify with the idealized image that people in their environment expect of them. They are little aware of this identification and confuse their authentic desires with those of the "character" they identify with.

NEUROTIC FEATURES:

SOCIAL SKILLS: enthusiastic, pleasant, ingenious, needs flattery. It adapts and blends into any environment in which it moves.

ORIENTATION TO SUCCESS: success, status, wealth and power. Desire to shine and excel.

NEED FOR ATTENTION, to be seen, heard, appreciated. It likes to attract or call attention.

Superficial, frivolous and adaptable image.

DISCONNECTION, little contact with your emotions and needs, can be very cold

PRAGMATIC, practice orientation.

Calculator and efficient.

CONTROL over oneself and over the other, falseness, manipulation.

CRAZY IDEAS:

"In this life they don't want you for who you are, but for what you do. You have to try hard to do things right. If they don't recognize me, it's because I don't have the courage. "

"I have to build the right image to be loved. I'm not worth it, only the mask is worth it. If I have success, prestige and admiration, then I will be happy. "

"If I am efficient, I will adapt and they will love me."

"The world is dangerous; you have to be vigilant and make sure they don't hurt me."

"Since I cannot bear rejection, I will refuse first"

"I need the gaze of the other to exist. If they don't confirm what I am I don't exist. "

"I have to deny my emotions and do what they expect me to do to be appreciated."

"If something happens to someone or something goes wrong, it means I haven't done things right."

HEALTHY IDEAS:

"I have to get away from the world, stop for a moment, look inside to connect with the essential and avoid the vain and the superficial. I have the right to meet my needs. "

"It's best to accept that whatever I do, you can't please everyone."

"You don't have to control and try so hard to be effective and make things perfect. Things will go as they should go and not everything depends on our control. "

"I can release the forced image I show of myself and show what I think and feel. If someone loves me, they can love me simply because I exist. "

"I can accept success and failure, pleasure and pain as a normal thing in life."

"I can be consistent with my emotions and my needs"

"The important thing is that I recognize myself and not depend too much on the recognition of others."

"I can count on authenticity and showing myself as I am, to be good for me and for others."

VIRTUE OF THE ENNEATYPE 3: AUTHENTICITY

Vanity is the need for pleasure. Authenticity would be showing oneself, being seen, freeing the image and not falsifying one's emotions and needs.

Let yourself be guided more by intuition and emotion without expecting to control everything so much. Bring attention to what you feel and act accordingly, truthfully, without self-deception. Act freely, be more consistent with your needs. Don't act just to please the other but give yourself time to connect with the inner voices.

Enneatype 3 conservation: accept criticism, release the image of perfection, allow yourself to make mistakes. Don't be so obsessed with security. Look more inwards and recognize yourself. Give yourself more pleasure without goals.

Enneatype 3 social aim: to try to be less vain. Its virtue lies in simplicity, in getting rid of the effort to keep the mask and not denying its genuine emotions and needs.

Sexual Enneatype 3: Stop seducing and accept that things happen more naturally. Less physical vanity. Release the image and simply try to "be". Stop and connect with your emotions, release fear.

HEALING ATTITUDES FOR THE ENNEATYPE 3

Enneatype 3 must be aware that healing necessarily passes through awareness of the role it tends to play. He plays it when he's with other people, but sometimes even when he's alone. This is because there is an unconscious identification with the ideal of the character he is playing. If, as Enneatype 3, you don't know exactly what you want to do, don't be scared and don't fall into the trap of following the script of your role. Be aware of your tendency to work tirelessly and the tiredness that this generates. You can't work and stress all day. Even if you think you can do it, your body can't, and if you don't give it rest you will suffer from stress-like and / or psychosomatic symptoms.

Rest is not "wasting time", but giving the body what it needs. Also, if your body is rested, it performs more and more efficiently than when you are under stress and anxiety. Meditation is a very suitable exercise for Enneatype 3. Meditation is very far from the concept of doing nothing. It is a space where the person can be himself, connect with his needs and benefit from the effects of slow and quiet ventral breathing. It is usually very difficult for people of this personality model to meditate and therefore it is very good for them to do so. Don't believe that people will only appreciate you for your strength, skills and effectiveness. When you are with trusted people it is very beneficial to you that you can show some of your vulnerabilities and fears. You will verify that you are well received and understood by others; you will probably be loved more if they see you as more "human".

ENNEAGRAM CONSERVATIVE SUBTYPE 3

STORAGE: the word is SAFETY because they try to feel and do all things with the maximum possible safety. They are workers, managers, assistants and always in action. They tend to build a comfort zone from which they interact. Of the 3 enneatypes, this subtype is the one that externally appears coldest, stiff and hard. They also seem less vain. They are said to be the anti-enneatype 3. They show a harmonious personality but without apparent arrogance. They don't show themselves emotionally in public (they don't show pain or sadness).

Remember all the details

It must always be very safe He is good at solving anything

He lives having everything resolved and struggles to maintain this position

They are specialists in solving situations for others and do not give themselves the time or opportunity to look at themselves.

It can be confused with the enneatype 4; conservation for perfectionism and the workload it assumes

He believes he can do everything with his efforts Labour intensive

He resembles Enneatype 1 where he is honest, meticulous, critical, hyper-ethical, obsessed with details and passionate about the idea of having to do the tasks perfectly

Enneatype 1 is restrained and serious and Enneatype 3 is more expansive and cheerful or neutral. The first is tradition-oriented and the second to the approval of the others

Avoid recognizing the pain and control its emotional expressions

He knows how to defend himself if necessary

SOCIAL SUB-TYPE OF THE ENNEAGRAM 3

SOCIAL: the word is PRESTIGE for the image of success they want to give to the company in the commitment to obtain prestige and social status.

They love power, work hard and deny their life. Organized, hardworking and capable. He doesn't like doing small things that go unnoticed, he likes doing big things that have social recognition. They like to interact with people who have social status and that society considers them "important".

They are chameleons. Their clothing and behavior depend on the environment they are in. They are more sociable, funny and fun, but they also have a lot of character.

In couple relationships they tend to be the ones who dominate the relationship. In their life story they can come from very humble origins and this becomes the engine of their ambition.

They can be confused with the social enneatype 2, but the latter wants to drive, while the social enneatype 3 prefers to be alongside the leader.

He hopes they love him for what he does

The vainest ==> search for prestige and fame ==> is the most mercenary

He wants to be someone important ==> very publicly recognized

Use socially accepted values by the piece

He wants to be known not so much for his looks as for what he does and his social status

Likes to move more, travel, know everything a little bit (can be confused with E7) Can be confused with social E2:

E2: wants to be loved. It is safer. He thinks he is special.

E3: must be recognized to feel important. Easily contacts with failure or insecurity without feedback from the other. Seeks attention from important people

His resource is ostentation ==> feeling of power and being respected and admired

He thinks he can make a living from his prestige. He's more of a liar. He falsifies his image to sell it. He doesn't do little things because it doesn't stimulate him, unless he has a return in results that confirm his desire to be someone important

In the sexual field he knows where he walks He takes power in the couple and is dominant

He is stronger, he can be tough and overwhelming. He is the most competitive

Believes what he sells

SEXUAL SUBTYPE OF THE ENNEAGRAM 3

SEXUAL: the word is ATTRACTION; they are so-called because they have a greater tendency to try to conquer others through their attractiveness. People of this subtype desire to feel wanted by others, but with the sole purpose of gaining recognition. One could say that "you can look but don't touch". Of the three subtypes of the enneatype 3, this is the one that has a greater tendency to be a little shyer, tender, insecure and sweet. In couple relationships they have a tendency not to be the ones who dominate the relationship. In sexual relations they put more energy into pleasing the other than into enjoying. He wants to be loved for his physical presence, charm and intimacy

He is the most shy, fragile and insecure

Puts more energy into the relationship with the opposite sex
He wants to give the ideal image

Send erotic messages but only to attract; he is not willing to deliver what he promises

He wants to be wanted but without being touched

He distinguishes sex from love and in sex he tries to please the other

Recognizing that he wants to be seen is taboo for him

His shyness is linked to the fear of showing that he is empty inside

He thinks he needs someone because he doesn't have enough resources

He may have problems at work because he is more oriented towards the other

In the sexual field he is bored with a stable partner In the sexual field he is irresponsible and innocent Leaves the power to his partner

He is afraid of getting into a relationship too much because he doesn't know what can happen

It is the most expressive, emotional and sweet They are not aggressive but they can get tough

THE ENNEATYPE 3 IN LOVE

They seem very confident people, but deep down (unconsciously) they are not. They need others' validation to feel good and safe. This is why they are always immersed in a mechanism where they depend on others (for the need to seduce them with their image and effectiveness) and at the same time they feel independent and secure when they dominate others (becoming dependent on them). Love must also be validated by others, so as to be put at his service. At the same time, while seducing the other with this love he gives, he wants to get the love of the other. They are people who find it difficult to truly believe in love because they believe that much of it is the result of their ability to seduce and dazzle through their appearance, not because they are the way they are. In this game or struggle in the field of love, his effort to be efficient diminishes his loving capacity. Dedicating so much energy to self-control and to his image makes it difficult for him to give himself to love, both to give it and to receive it. Love can become secondary to work or success; of minor importance.

HOW TO BEHAVE WITH THE ENNEATYPE 3

Be effective and don't seek his approval, don't waste his time and get to the point. He's busy. Arrive prepared on what you want to say and if you can, provide an outline and argue with data. What matters are the results and action points. Don't be a hindrance to him and don't hinder him. Respect what you said you will do to let him know that you are engaged to him. If you don't do your part, he will punish you. What he likes most is effectiveness. Let him know everything he does well because his goal is to gain recognition. He likes to get tangible results. Don't compete with him, it's better to cooperate with him. If you work well, don't expect him to thank you, he considers it your duty.

How to get along with Enneatype 3:

Leave me alone while I do my job

Help me keep my environment harmonious and peaceful Tell me how you are with me

Tell me when you are proud of me or of my achievements Be honest with me, but not too critical

What I like about being an Enneatype 3:

Being optimistic and kind

Being able to recover quickly from the blows of life Knowing what's going on

Being competent and able to make things work efficiently

Being able to motivate people

The difficult part of being an ennea type 3: Having to endure inefficiency and incompetence

The fear of not being (or not being seen) as successful Confronting the people who make things better Struggle for my success

Appearing to impress people Always being "on". It's exhausting

As children, individuals of Enneatype 3 tend to: Work hard to gain recognition for their achievements

They get along very well with other children and adults

They are some of the most capable and responsible children in their class or school

They are active in school and club governance or are quietly busy working on their own projects

Enneatype 3 as a parent:

They are consistent, trustworthy and loyal

They struggle between the desire to spend time with their children and to do more professional work

They expect their children to be responsible and organized

Chapter 5

Enneatype 4 Artist

People corresponding to this model tend to have a bad image of themselves. Even if they are successful in life and may feel superior to others, there is always a sense of lack. A feeling of being a member of the "true aristocracy", but with deep feelings of shame and fear of being somehow deeply flawed. Enneatype 4 people tend to build their identities around the idea that they are quite different or unique people. They tend to see their difference from others as a gift and a curse at the same time. A gift, because it differentiates them "from the bunch" and a curse because it often takes them away from enjoying happiness in a simple way. Those who belong to enneatype 4 are emotionally complex and highly sensitive.

They yearn to be understood and appreciated for their true selves, but they feel easily misunderstood and underappreciated. They tend to have a bit of a bad temper. They spend much of their life immersed in their inner mental landscapes, where they feel free to cultivate and analyze their feelings. To manifest this internal world, Enneatype 4 tends to have an interest in the arts and some become real artists. Whether artistic or not, however, most of those who fall into this group are aesthetically sensitive and concerned with self-expression and self-disclosure, whether in the clothes they wear, or the general nature of their style. of life. They are a little melancholy and tend to get depressed. When they are unbalanced, they easily give way to a complacency which they perceive as something fully justified to compensate for the general lack of pleasure they experience in their life. Instead of seeking practical solutions to their difficulties, they are inclined to fantasize about a savior who will save them from their unhappiness

KEY MOTIVES FOR ENNEATYPE 4:

They want to express their uniqueness, to create and surround themselves with beauty, to maintain certain moods and feelings. They are not satisfied with their image. They want to attract a "savior".

WHEN ENNEATYPE 4 IS HEALTHIER:

He knows how to attract others by his sensitivity and orientation to beauty, and tries to give everything an artistic and original touch. He seeks intense experiences and is very in touch with his inner world. He experiences feelings very intensely and has the ease of contacting the feelings of others.

HEALTHY ATTITUDES OF THE ENNEATYPE 4

The neurotic introspection of Enneatype 4 can generate strong feelings and negative emotions about themselves in these people. If your personality model matches this enneatype, you need to be aware of this tendency to devalue yourself emotionally. Don't justify these negative emotions, they are false! Do not look for arguments that explain these feelings because you will find them, but they are not true, they are a hypothesis that tries to "adapt" past events to present feelings. Always keep in mind that you have a tendency to interpret events from a somewhat negative perspective. But just because you hear it doesn't mean it's the truth!

People of this personality pattern are used to having great sensitivity, but emotional fickleness and rapid mood swings don't match that sensitivity. Rapid reactions to the small actions of others or the environment tend to prevent experiences from being lived more fully and deeply. Sometimes, paradoxically, these rapid emotional reactions indicate a fear of exploring the deepest and most true feelings.

As for your alleged weaknesses, seek feedback from your closest friends and trust their opinion. If they are being honest with you, you have to believe them; don't think they are saying something positive just to cheer you up. Be aware that your thirst for attention and affection may never end. You can ask for attention and affection from your loved ones or closest friends, but don't overdo it. You will tend to feel that you do not have enough of this attention and affection, and then it is possible that the reactions will require more. If you do not become aware of this neurotic attitude of asking in a subtle but constant way, you can oppress the people closest to you and make them turn away. Just because your loved ones love you doesn't mean they have to / can put up with your emotional ups and downs or that your problems are more serious than theirs.

CONSERVATIVE: Of the three subtypes these are the strongest, the least emotional, the most intellectual, the most introverted and the least complaining. Their main distinguishing feature is their great effort, discipline and perseverance (they may resemble enneatype 1 in this sense). For this TENACITY is a trait that suits him. They are people who ask a lot of themselves, more than others. They impose a system of needs that are difficult to satisfy. Nothing is enough, they always have to keep trying a little harder. They tend to suffer in silence. They focus their envy and hypersensitivity in their immediate environment. They find security and tranquility in beauty and aesthetics.

They try to appease their emotional states by surrounding themselves and allowing themselves satisfactions, beautiful objects, their favorite meals, sex, or any other object / activity that can serve to "compensate" their sense of internal suffering (with a certain tendency towards luxury and 'exclusive'). For example, after a stressful situation, they may react by going to have a massage, a spa or a quality wine. Small rewards are given to "compensate" for their suffering state of mind. Emotionally they are very sensitive to the small details of their environment. For example, the light in the room, the temperature, the smell, the fabric of the sofa, the music, etc.

For them all of this has symbolic meaning and can cause an emotional response. They can intensely connect a sensation to an object. They may feel that losing a donated item is like losing the friend who gave them that gift. They can keep apparently obsolete objects for many years. They can be very temperamental to buy items, for example wanting to buy the bag they saw in a small Paris shop during the summer. They can also be difficult to satisfy with a gift (because it is not exactly as they imagined). Their envy is the result of a negative self-image. They have a bad concept of themselves, their characteristics and everything they have.

For this reason, they consider others to be better than them. His envy does not respond to the gluttony of wanting to have more and better, but responds to a feeling of not being able to be satisfied with his alleged shortcomings; they may believe they are unacceptable to others. This is why they try so hard to be "special", to show that they know how to appreciate a good wine or select the most beautiful dress. They don't want to sound vulgar. They usually take care of their image: clothes, hairstyles, etc. Because of their interest in the image and their need, they can suffer from eating disorders. People of this subtype are very emotionally intense. They can create intense situations unconsciously, but they often desire and seek it. Sometimes, to find this intensity, they can take unnecessary risks (similar to sexual enneatype 6).

They can look for challenges that make them feel alive and even take risks as a form of aggression to the other: "If something happens to me it will be his fault and he will feel responsible." Due to their emotional intensity and their unconventional mood, they can react aggressively and with little awareness. Due to their low self- esteem and low mood, some people of this personality model may be convinced that they cannot, or that their disorders hinder them from having a "normal job".

When they are more balanced, they can focus, work hard and be decisive at work, a cause they strongly believe in, or their goals. They are good at managing their money and their assets. They can have great aesthetic sensibility and express it artistically. They are good at looking from a different perspective than the conventional one. When they are less centered, they may take excessive risks to emotionally cover the emotional emptiness they feel they have or to attract the attention of their closest neighbors. They may try too hard to give an image to look "special". They are very sensitive to minor inconveniences or criticisms from others. Sometimes they believe that no one understands their suffering. They can be indulgent with bad habits to compensate for their emotional state (food, drink, sex, luxury, etc.).

ENNEATYPE 4 SOCIAL

They have an idealized image of themselves in the negative. They feel that they are somehow flawed and that others will never love them or value them. They feel inferior and trapped in a situation that has no solution; "I will always be inferior to others". They can be very self-critical and ashamed to consider that they deviate from what they believe are the standards of the group. They are used to being very sensitive to criticism. They are ashamed of being as they are, which is why the characteristic of SHAME is associated with this subtype. It is as if they have unconsciously registered the feeling of

"I'm defective and the group knows it". They remain with the suffering; they do not contemplate improvements. They are romantic. After the individuals of enneatype 9, they are the most masochistic.

Of the three subtypes of Enneatype 4, the social subtype is the most emotional and the one that most externally shows its spiritual state. They have a tendency to want to induce pity with the aim of manipulation. They make themselves wanted but they are not sincere. They try to get what they want from others out of pity. For this they immerse themselves in a vicious circle where they show that they feel bad in order to pity others so that they can get what they want from them. As social subtypes, they focus their envy and hypersensitivity in the social sector. They wish to belong to a glamorous social group, but they feel unable.

They believe they will hardly be accepted as they are. They tend to feel closer to those who seem to be excluded. People of the social subtype are the most extroverted of Enneatype 4. They can hide the extent of their feelings of social inadequacy and be funny. They love to show their style and sense of aesthetics. They tend to work hard to create an image through which they relate. This public image they try to offer is more optimistic and happier with how they really feel. Unlike Enneatype 3, they have the awareness of representing a character. Sometimes they can fantasize about being rejected without anyone having spoken yet and showing a hostile attitude as a preventive defense.

They may find it difficult to keep a job due to their tendency to feel excluded and to build a relationship of loneliness among their colleagues (it is in their best interest to have a small social network to support them). When they are more centered, with their great intuition and sensitivity they can develop excellent social skills. They are generous and care about the well-being of the group they are part of and the people close to them. They may have enough self-esteem to interact with the group, but not get carried away by it.

When they are less balanced, they suffer between the desire to want to fit in and be accepted, but to be special and unique. They may want to reinforce your image with an extreme look. They stop doing things for fear of being humiliated or rejected; they can isolate themselves or become antisocial. They are hypersensitive to criticism.

SEXUAL subtype

They are probably among the most intense characters (they can be confused with the enneatype 8). Their intensity is a gift and a curse. The word HATE is associated with them because they are people who tend to energetically project the guilt of their discomfort outwards. They focus their envy and hypersensitivity in their intimate relationships. They have a great ability, sensitivity, and desire to cultivate deep intimacy. They invest a lot of energy in the person they want. They attach great importance to the loving part of their life and believe that when they find perfect love, they will be happy.

They may have a crush on someone they've seen a couple of times. They may also be attracted to people who possess qualities and talents that they believe they lack, with the (unconscious) intention of becoming more complete (this rarely works). They are romantic, they are attracted to what they cannot have, they are looking for someone special or someone to "save" them from this world where they are not seen or understood.

They may think that life is meaningless without the person they love. They tend to have high expectations of people close to them. They go through great sentimental changes and feelings towards their loved ones; they can go from idolizing to hating. They are very polar, rapidly rising and falling. They idealize the couple, but they destroy it for small things. When they stop idealizing the person they are with, they begin to find "flaws" in them, used as a pretext to get angry with them. When the person is absent, they may be eager to get back to her, but when they do, they may get angry with her for "whatever reason". They tend to have love-hate relationships.

They are used to being aware of their emotional states, even negative ones, which they can sometimes express in a self-destructive way. They can be jealous of their partner, even their past relationships. They are very competitive. Competitiveness is based on the "envious" confrontations they make with their close friends. They are competitive in personal relationships and tend to be a bit into everything, also being able to emphasize their competitiveness on a professional level. They are very strong and action-oriented people. It could be said that their competitiveness is not so much focused on "I will win", but on "I will make you lose". They may not be able to enjoy their successes without degrading the successes of others.

They can be sensual and warm, but also unpleasant. On the inside they feel they are worthless and, on the outside, they despise the other, even going so far as to ask him to go to hell to show him their love. And if the other doesn't care, they interpret that this is because they don't love them enough. Suffering is important to them. A person who does not suffer is a person who is not worthy. For them there is always guilt, this is their reason for living.

They can be unbearable, when they become unbearable and the other separates from them, then they confirm their fears: "See! You don't really love me". Their self-esteem is not based on themselves, but is nurtured by the love of their partner and intimate. When sexual type 4 is more balanced, it is able to deeply admire and love the partner, accepting their own uniqueness. They can engage deeply with people, in an authentic and passionate way. They are capable of being extremely open-hearted, compassionate and loving towards all. They can develop excellent communication skills and interpersonal relationships.

When people of this subtype are less centered, they may desire an impossible or unavailable partner, and believe that this is the only way to have love. They idealize their partner and place very high expectations on these, which will not come true and will arouse anger. The typical relationship with the partner is one of love-hate.

They can be seductive, sexual, jealous and possessive. They can be overly competitive, especially on romantic themes.

THE ENNEATYPE 4 IN LOVE

People of Enneatype 4 are characterized by a sense of lack and a bad image of themselves. When a person does not love himself, it is difficult for him to have a good relationship with others. These people tend to underestimate themselves and believe they are rejected. For this reason, with this firmly rooted belief in rejection, they can modify their behavior in order to achieve genuine rejection. And if they feel loved, they come to ask themselves, "Why does he love me if I'm awful?" So, they can devalue the other. In the field of love, they are passionate, but it is a romantic and melancholy love which they connect to suffering. This passion can become addiction and insatiability.

Being so passionate about love has negative consequences for them, because they may tend to demand more urgently than the other can give them, and this tends to produce negative consequences. It is also characteristic of this enneatype to ask with the aim of "making pity", showing suffering, their role as victim or their illnesses. It is an "emotional blackmail" that can also appear in family relationships. These people tend to demand a lot of themselves, suffer a lot and have no mercy on themselves.

HOW TO TREAT THE ENNEATYPE 4

Admire his aesthetic ability

He doesn't like rigid goals. Bonuses and rewards for doing something leave him indifferent. Let me explain things in his own way. Enneatype 4 likes to feel special and that their uniqueness is appreciated.

It can be stimulated by showing him the particularity of his contribution. Don't belittle his feelings. Don't ask him to be positive or "smile" because he will lock himself in even more.

Accept that he is a mysterious person, that he is intense. Tell him what you see creativity in his suggestions. Because they tend to feel abandoned, make your promises clear to them and keep them.

Chapter 6

The Enneatype 5 Observer

The void in the lower part of the Enneagram indicates a decisive change in existential attitude between the positions marked in point Four and point Five. If, in fact, the Four is, as we have seen, marked by an ardent desire and by the hope of being able to change its state, the Five is deeply convinced that nothing can change for the better.

Type five are children who have seen the world as it is, not being able to understand it (not even the vast majority of adults can) have erected barriers to save themselves. He tends to be an introverted person, quiet, objective, impassive and self-sufficient, not very affable and very afraid, even if his attitude is more detached than intimidated. In addition to this he almost always had to compete with forces enormously superior to his own and unlike the type eight that has imposed itself, the type five has retired. Type Fives are sharp, intuitive, inquisitive, and manage to engage and focus on developing complex ideas and skills.

They are independent, innovative and inventive, but they can also let themselves be absorbed by their own imaginary thoughts and elaborations and become detached, while remaining hypersensitive and intense. They typically have problems with eccentricity, nihilism and isolation. Personality type Five. The Investigator, because more than any other type he wants to find out why things are the way they are. The Five want to understand how the world works, be it the cosmos, the microscopic, animal, vegetable, mineral world or the world of their imagination.

They are always on the lookout, asking questions and delving into things in detail.

They do not accept preconceived opinions or doctrines and feel a strong need to experience the truth of many assumptions for themselves. Behind their relentless pursuit of knowledge lies deep insecurities about their ability to succeed in life. Fives feel they don't know how to do things as well as others. But instead of engaging in activities that might boost their confidence, they "step back" and take refuge in their mind, where they feel most capable.

Their belief is that from that safe place that is their mind they will eventually figure out how to do things so that they can one day reunite with the world. The Five spend a lot of time observing and contemplating, listening to the sound of the wind or a synthesizer, taking notes on the activities of an anthill in their yard. As they immerse themselves in their observations, they begin to internalize their knowledge and gain a feeling of self-confidence.

Then they can go out and play a piece on the synthesizer or tell people what they know about ants. They can also come across new and exciting information or produce new and creative combinations of sounds (playing a piece of music based on the recording of the sound produced by wind and water). When they get a verification of their observations and hypotheses or see that others understand their work, it is a confirmation of their competence and it satisfies their Basic Desire ("To know what one is talking about").

History is full of famous Fives who have overturned accepted ways of understanding and doing things (Einstein, Nietzsche). However, most Fives get lost in the Byzantine complexities of their mental processes, leaving room for eccentricity and social isolation. The high concentration of Fives can therefore lead to considerable breakthroughs and innovations, but when the personality is more fixed it can also create counterproductive problems. This is because their concentration serves to distract them from their most pressing practical problems. Whatever the sources of their anxieties, relationships, lack of physical strength, not finding work, and so on,

Mid-Level Fives tend not to address these issues. Rather, they find something else that makes them feel more competent. The irony is that no matter what degree of mastery they develop in their area of expertise, it cannot resolve the fundamental insecurities regarding their functioning in the world.

For example, as a marine biologist a Type Five can learn everything there is to know about a type of mollusk, but if his fear is that he will never be able to manage his family properly, that will not solve his underlying anxiety. Handling material things directly can be nerve-wracking for Fives. The problem is that while they are absorbed in this process, they are not interacting with others nor are they developing other practical and social skills.

They devote more and more time to collecting and dealing with what they have collected and less and less to anything related to their real needs. So the challenge of Fives is to understand that they can seek answers to any topic or problem that fires their imagination and at the same time maintaining relationships with others, really taking care of themselves and doing all those things that are essential for a healthy life Type Five is particularly jealous of his privacy, he needs his own well-defined space to take refuge to recover energy and reflect, it can be the isolated house or a favorite armchair.

The retreat allows him to retrace past and future events as well as to restore order to his thoughts and feelings, this is because he is unable to respond immediately about what he feels or thinks, it takes time before externalizing what they feel or giving a accurate answer. In this type we find more for logic and rationality and consequently most of the geniuses of the history of humanity to which only the type seven is second, a type connected as we will see later.

Commitments and opportunities are seen as threats to their attempt to keep a safe distance, it is more reassuring to refuse a threatening commitment than to be involved in situations potentially capable of opening doors in their protection to the weakness they think they have. The state of need of the five is buried deeply in the psyche, behind a veil of indifference, resignation and stoic renunciation. The taboo is not only in satisfying them, but even in recognizing them.

His inability to give is manifested in his strategy towards the world: he distances himself and renounces the relationship with others, these people are described as cold, isolated, autistic and schizoid. In avarice the (unacknowledged) desire is expressed through the ability to "hold back", a "holding back" that hides the catastrophic fantasy that letting go would mean total emptying. The fear of impending poverty is also what is the background to the impulse to accumulate. In addition to the tendency to hold back, we also find renunciation too easy: the 5, resigned to not obtaining the love of others, compensates by clinging to himself, and / or material things and adapts to an economy of minimum effort and maximum resource saving.

The taboo for 5 is greed which is often unconscious, as quick-tempered people are often unaware of the anger they harbor within. He lives with an undertone of general threat to his inner life and his isolation and self-control take the form of some sort of petrification. If the perfectionist is an active extrovert and criticizes the outside world, in 5 perfection is cultivated within himself: it is the thought-type introvert who avoids action.

Unlike the 1 which is demanding and identifies with the super-ego self-coherent, the 5 tries to minimize his own needs and demands and identifies itself with the oppressed and guilty sub-personality, object of the super-ego's requests, for this reason it is ready to be commanded by it.

Inability to give: it manifests itself in avoiding involvement and in the parallel need to be completely free and released which is associated with hypersensitivity to the feeling of being submerged. In the tendency to accumulate we not only find the manifestation of avarice, but also the prevention of remaining lacking in the necessary in the future.

Pathological detachment: He is not affected by his loneliness, he is a true loner because he is resigned to not having relationships, which he perpetuates through emotional detachment and removing the need for others (thus minimizing the other).

Fear of being submerged: avoid others for fear of being swallowed up, fear of dependence, fear that in the relationship with others he may not express his preferences which give rise to the implicit tension and the need to recover them by being alone.

Autonomy: having removed the need to establish relationships with others, he must do without external resources and therefore he talks about it by idealizing autonomy, thus reinforcing the removal of desires: "I can think, I can wait, I can fast" (Siddhartha

Herman Hesse)

Insensitivity: it removes needs, represses anger, is "insensitive" in the sense that it not only loses awareness of feelings, but interferes with their arising since it avoids both their expression and their implementation. Even the ability to rejoice seems to be absent, in fact pleasure is "postponed" to give way to more urgent impulses such as maintaining the safe distance between oneself and others and the desire for autonomy.

Postponement of the action: to act means to commit oneself, to use one's energies, to feel enthusiasm, to express one's intentions ... all this clashes with the indifferent attitude of the 5 which therefore inhibits one's activity and does not develop spontaneous gestures and initiative and structures a excessive control. This postponing action can be considered a hybrid between negativism and avoidance of action.

Cognitive orientation: with intellectualism not only does he find substitute satisfaction, but he prepares himself for life because he typically never feels ready and, given that action is inhibited with abstraction, he manages to avoid concreteness ... rather than live the life, he becomes a witness, a detached observer, even if acute.

Sense of emptiness: withdrawal from relationships and resorting to intellectual life (for which he is very gifted by nature) results in the sense of emptiness and lack of meaning typical of the 5 (even if the dominant passion in all character structures leads always to an ontic insufficiency).

Guilt: like 4, 5 also tends to guilt that stems through the distance which, as we have said, is the precocious and implicit decision taken to react to the lack of love on the part of the outside world. This guilt manifests itself as a vague sense of inferiority, vulnerability to intimidation, awkwardness and embarrassment. The cold detachment of the 5 is comparable to the typical anger of the 8, but since in the 5 the anger struggles to express itself, it manifests itself as an opposition, a hostile contempt, an isolation from others which, however, he feels a sense of guilt.

A demanding super-ego: 1 is consistent with the super-ego and is therefore demanding, the 5 is very demanding with itself, but identifies with the devalued self.

Negativism: when he chooses to do something out of an authentic desire, once it takes the form of a project, it risks becoming a "should", he loses motivation. All this corresponds to a form of internal rebellion, to a desire to sabotage one's own and others' requests, not to do what is deemed necessary.

Hypersensitivity: manifests itself in a whole range of behaviors ranging from poor pain tolerance to fear of rejection. Emotional numbness seems to be a defense against hypersensitivity.

The lack of the dimension of pleasure and the feeling of not worth seem to lower the pain threshold that a 5 can endure and his hypersensitivity can be considered as one of the factors that determine his decision to avoid the pain of frustrating relationships, choosing the isolation and autonomy.

Defensive mechanisms

The predominant mechanism is isolation, interconnected to a more primitive one, the splitting of the ego. The subject detaches himself from the emotional life and from the affections up to a physical isolation from others and is led to live each separate experience by interposing a void between one and the other and thus losing sight of the context that gives a complete meaning. In childhood it is a bit as if character five had forgotten a very weak bond with his mother and had thus developed isolation and distance. About the split in the ego there coexist in him a grandiose ego that alternates with an insignificant ego, these two parts of the ego do not know each other and the person is induced to pass from one to the other, to separate his vision of reality and to perceive things in a positive and negative way at the same time by not becoming aware of the contradiction.

Subtypes Conservative

The conservative subtype is the most isolated and autistic, it is led to idealize its lair and consequently it also idealizes itself (for example, in Kafka's stories). The mechanism of isolation is active: the subject seems to forget the world to defend himself from any pain, frustration and to protect himself from the invasion of the desires of others. He does everything to hide, to become invisible even to himself.

Social

The social subtype, in addition to the mechanism of isolation and splitting, uses primitive idealization, is the tendency to create totems, to make some people almost divine, this leads them to always see the best of others and to devalue themselves and who it is not up to the totem poles. Character five oscillates at the same time in the identification between a grandiose and denigrated image and conceives the world as inhabited by a few special beings and many worthless and uninteresting people.

Sexual

The sexual subtype is a romantic: on the one hand it is looking for love, on the other it feels its emptiness, its lack. As in the social subtype, idealization is the search for the totem, the sexual one searches for an ideal of love that has its roots in the idealization of women.

Chapter 7

Enneatype 6 The Collaborator

The subject in question is the emblem of contradiction. He is: the loyalist, the guardian, the true believer, the doubter, the flaw seeker, the traditionalist. This type is security oriented; he is responsible, anxious, suspicious. The basic fear is: a lack of self-confidence and therefore the fear of having no support and guidance and therefore of being unable to survive on one's own. Basically, this character is characterized by an underlying cowardice and shyness that can be interpreted as an anxious hesitation or an inhibition of action due to fear.

Basic desire: to find safety and support.

Superego message is: you are good if you do what is expected of you.

The compulsive message is: "I am trustworthy and obey orders, even if others don't.

Their virtue is courage as counterphobic behavior.

The temptation is to be dependent on others and therefore do not focus their energy on building adequate self-esteem. When they are not under stress, they show courage and are able to fight to the last.

Character and neurosis

There is no doubt that the human needs to be met for the individual to become an adult in full possession of his functions are very complex, and there are many things that may not go the right way; or, if we want to put it differently, the need to receive the necessary love from parents can be frustrated or betrayed in many ways. Sometimes parents are so engrossed that they are negligent; at other times the excessive need to take sides with adults compromises the child's experience; at other times, the shadow of violence can weigh on tenderness, and so on.

Let's say that our way of living in this "low" world after the expulsion from Eden (ie the personality with which we identify and which we implicitly refer to when we say "I") is a way of being that we have adopted to defend ourselves and our well-being thanks to an adaptation, in a broad sense, which is generally tinged with rebellion rather than acceptance. In order to react to the lack of what he needed, the child had to resort to manipulation, and therefore, from this point of view, we can say that character is a counter-manipulation apparatus.

This being the case, life is not guided by instinct, but by the persistence of an early adaptive strategy that fights against instinct and interferes with the wisdom of the organism in the broadest sense of the term. The persistence of this early adaptive strategy can be understood in light of the painful context in which it originated, and the particular type of learning that feeds it: not what the evolving organism assimilates for free, but learning under coercion, characterized by a special fixity or rigidity of the behavior initially adopted as an emergency reaction.

So, let's say that the individual is no longer free to choose whether or not to apply the results of the new learning, but that he has gone into "automatic", initiating a series of reactions without "consulting" the mind as a whole, or without considering the situation in a creative way. The fixity of such obsolete responses and the loss of the ability to creatively react to the present are typical of psychopathological functioning.

To the total sum of these pseudo-adaptive learning, in general, we give the name of "I" or "personality" or more closely to the reason that leads us to this seminar, we give the name of "character" which means "to sculpt" and it refers to what remains constant in the person, because it is engraved within him, and therefore to behavioral, emotional and cognitive conditioning. We observe that in psychoanalysis the fundamental model of neurosis is that of an instinctual life bounded by the activity of the super-ego internalized by the external world, while here we will advance the hypothesis that the basic conflict, and therefore the fundamental way of disagreeing with ourselves, arises from the interference of the character on the self-regulation of the organism.

Character has a fundamental core in which a dual nature can be distinguished: the dominant passion and the dominant cognitive style (fixation). These, metaphorically, represent the focal points of an ellipse that condition the growth process through the interference of passion fueled by the influence of a distorting cognitive tendency. The 6 have difficulty in contacting their inner guide; therefore, they have a lack of self-confidence. Let's see their childhood path: The 6 lost faith in authority in childhood.

They fearfully remember the power exercised over them and the inability to act in their own interests.

These memories (unconscious or still conscious) feed into adult life an attitude of suspicion towards the motives of others. Their basic fear (of being without support and guidance, and of being unable to survive on their own) is a very real and universal fear in every child. A child cannot live without mum and dad; the child is completely dependent on them. Clear memories of the terror related to this addiction are etched into most people, but at some point, in their development, children who are learning to walk do a remarkable thing.

In spite of their tremendous dependence, they begin to distance themselves from their mother, to assert their independence and autonomy. In child psychology, this is called the separation phase. One of the most important ingredients that helps the child find the courage to separate from the mother is the presence of the father figure. This is not always the biological father, although it often is. He is the person who provides discipline, structure and authority in the family. If the father figure is present in a consistent way, then it becomes a guide and support for the child's desire for independence. It teaches the child what the ways of living in the world are - what is sure and what is not - becomes the essential support and inner guidance of the child.

Of course, for many of us, this process happened in a far less than perfect way, giving rise to our own insecurities as adults. But while everyone experiences this to some degree, the subjects in question remain particularly stuck on this. Furthermore, if the child perceives that the father's support for his independence is insufficient, he may feel in danger of being overwhelmed by the mother and what she represents to him. This increases the need to keep on guard and leads to the subject's deep ambivalence. They therefore experience the contradiction we have already mentioned: they desire approval and closeness and at the same time want to be supported but not overwhelmed.

To solve this dilemma, they make an alliance with the father figure, but this usually leads them to ambivalent behavior - the father figure seems too tight and in control or too little supportive and uninteresting. Some of these subjects end up making a difficult compromise: they offer external obedience while continuing to maintain a feeling of independence with acts of inner rebellion and alternate large and small acts of passivity with large and small acts of aggression. The six act in fits and starts. Their life is full of job changes and interrupted projects. It is as if they are afraid to act in their interests. And when a project is about to be realized, anxiety increases the closer the target is.

The defense mechanisms: phobia and counterphobia

Its defense mechanisms are: identification, displacement, projection.

Projection, for this character, is the most pervasive defense mechanism. In severe cases of psychopathological states, this character can take the psycho-paranoid form with persecution mania. The six may have two different paranoid structures: the phobic and the counterphobic. The phobic six resembles the character implemented by Woody Allen, hesitates, replaces action with analysis, full of contradiction and self-doubt. The counterphobic six acts by throwing himself into the fray not out of courage but because he is unable to face the fear of his own ghosts.

Let's see more in depth what are the defense mechanisms of the six:

Procrastination of action: thought replaces action Difficulty getting a job done.

Omission of success and pleasure.

Problems with authority, which result in submission or rebellion.

Suspicion for the hidden motives of others, especially of authority.

Identification with the lost causes.

Loyalty to the cause of the underdog or strong leader. Fear of one's anger, of which others are blamed.

Doubt and skepticism.

Thorough examination of the environment in search of evidence that justifies the inner feeling of threat.

Intuition based on powerful imagination and powerful concentration, both of the fearful mind.

The weakness of the six is that it already has an opinion before looking for evidence and clues. For a six it is extremely difficult to recognize the difference between the habit of examining the environment to feel safe and examining the environment in search of evidence that confirms his point of view.

The trait that immediately emerges among these personality types is loyalty to friends and to the people they believe in. They are loyal to ideas, systems and beliefs, even to the belief that all ideas and all authorities can be questioned or defeated. Obviously not everyone accepts tano the status quo: their beliefs can be rebellious, anti-authoritarian and even revolutionary. In any case, they will generally fight for what they believe more fiercely than they would like to fight for themselves, and they will defend their community or family more tenaciously than they would defend themselves. The reason they are so loyal to others is that they don't want to be abandoned and left unsupported.

They are led to believe that they do not have the internal resources to face life's whims and challenges and so increasingly rely on structures, allies, those who believe the same; that is, they lean outside of themselves, relying on a guide. If there are no suitable structures, they will try to create and maintain them. As a result, they have little faith in their mind and judgment. Membership of an ideological group does not mean that they do not think. On the contrary, they think and worry a lot! They also have a tendency not to make important decisions, although at the same time they have resistance to letting someone else decide for them. They dislike being controlled, but they are also afraid of taking responsibility for themselves. They are always aware of their anxieties and are always looking for ways to "build social security" that are bulwarks against them. If they realize they have sufficient following they can advance with some degree of confidence. But if this crumbles they become anxious and self-doubt, awakening their basic fear ("I have to do it alone! What should I do then?"). A good question could therefore be: "How will I know I have enough security?" or, "what is security?" Without their essential inner guidance and the deep sense of support that this guidance brings, the 6 will have to constantly struggle to find solid ground.

They try to build a web of security, of faith on a basis of instability and fear. Therefore, they are often filled with nameless anxiety and then try to find or create reasons for doing. Wanting to feel that there is something solid and clear in their lives, they become attached to explanations and positions that seem to clarify their situation. Since "believing" is difficult for them and because their sense of stability is so important, once they establish a reliable belief, they no longer question it, and defend it at any cost.

The same thing happens for the important people in the life of these subjects. When they feel they can believe in someone, they latch on for a long time to maintain connections with the person who appears to be like a sounding board, a regulator of their emotional reactions and behavior. They therefore do whatever is in their power to keep this affiliation of theirs always alive.

Enneatype 6 fears deviating from group norms and defends itself by projecting unacceptable emotions onto others. Fear is one of the two passions that do not belong to the traditional list of sins or deadly vices. This was probably due to two different reasons. On the one hand, from a medieval Christian point of view, fear, or the fear of God, was not considered a negative element, since it, through the memory of the judgment of eternal punishment, led man to submit to the law and the social order. On the other hand, it must be said that the very dynamics of this passion were not well understood. The truth of fear-induced behaviors is such that, at first glance, there seems to be little in common among many people belonging to this enneatype. If, it is quite easy to understand that insecure or phobic people are dominated by fear; it is not so easy to see fear at work in those people called counterphobics, who act with a strong strategic aggression. In fact, when a 6 is with his back to the wall he reacts counterphobically. This reaction is not due to courage, but to an instinctive defense that is put into action by fear.

The fearful, in general, are very cerebral people, in the sense that they think too much about the possible repercussions of each of their individual acts, and fight their insecurity by requesting support and support and through a tendency to prefigure every possible scenario. For this reason, it is crucial to know what the behavior required by the authority is and, with their typical ambivalence, to know how to behave in the face of the requests that come from it. We will thus have three distinct behaviors that have, however, in common the fact that they all originate from the need to suppress fear. Unlike a five, a six hasn't parted ways with his feelings and desires, but doesn't know if he can trust them (meaning he is never sure of the reactions others will have), or if he can express them freely.

Chapter 8:

Enneatype 7 The Hedonist

He was a child who fragmented fear by taking refuge in the unlimited possibilities of the imagination. This typology is primarily focused on escaping pain. They hardly have sad childhood memories, in the sense that pain is separated from their own experiences. Type seven always sees the bright side of things, not to see the pain. So, if we ask a Seven of their childhood memories, they will immediately go to pleasant episodes. Then the moment we bring it to something negative it will tend to "sterilize" the experience from pain. Often this operation is carried out through a shift from the "lived experience" to the attitude, so not a "how bad I was", but a "I understood that I would never do it again". Although Seven types are in the Mind Center, this is not immediately apparent as they tend to be extremely practical and engaged in a multitude of projects all the time. Their thinking is anticipatory: they predict events and generate ideas "on the fly", encouraging activities that stimulate their mind and which in turn generate even more things to do and think about. Seven types are not necessarily intellectuals or scholars in the strict sense of the term, although they are often very intelligent and can read a lot and be very talkative.

Their mind quickly passes from one idea to another, making them gifted in the "brainstorming" process and in synthesizing information. The Seven are enhanced by the influx of ideas and the pleasure of being spontaneous, preferring broad views and the emotion of the initial moments of the creative process to the deepening of a single topic. The Seven are often endowed with quick and agile minds and are often exceptionally fast in learning. This is true both in their ability to absorb new information (foreign languages, notions, procedures), and in their ability to learn new manual skills. They tend to have excellent mind-body coordination and manual dexterity (typing, playing the piano, playing tennis). All this makes type Seven the quintessence of the "Renaissance persona". Ironically, their wide-ranging curiosity and ability to learn quickly can also create problems for them. Because they can learn many things relatively easily, it becomes difficult for them to decide what to do with themselves. As a result, they don't always value their skills as they would if they had to sweat to get them. However, when the Seven are more balanced their versatility, curiosity and learning ability lead them to achieve extraordinary results.

The root of their problem is common to all types of the Mental Center: the loss of contact with the inner guidance and support of their own Essence. As with types Five and Six, this creates deep anxiety in types Seven. They do not feel that they know what to do or how to make choices that can benefit themselves and others. Seven types deal with this anxiety in two ways: the first is by trying to keep their mind busy all the time; as long as they manage to keep their minds busy, especially with positive projects and ideas for the future, they can at least to a certain extent keep anxiety and negative feelings out of their sphere of awareness.

At the same time, since their thinking is stimulated by activity, they are forced to stay on the move, moving from one experience to another, always looking for new stimuli. This does not mean that they feel they are wasting time, on the contrary, they love to be concrete and able to attend to many chores. Secondly, the Seven manage the loss of Essential guidance using the "trial and error" method, they try everything to make sure they know what is best for them. On a deep level, the Seven don't feel they can find what they really want in their life. They therefore tend to try everything and eventually even resort to anything that can replace what they are really looking for. ("If I can't have what really satisfies me,

I'll enjoy it anyway. I'll have all kinds of experiences, so I don't feel bad about not finding what I really want"). On their positive side, Seven types are extremely optimistic, exuberant, and energetic people. They are endowed with abundant vitality and a great desire to live their life fully every day. They are naturally cheerful and in a good mood and tend not to take themselves or anything too seriously. As we have seen, the Fundamental Desire of the Seven types are to be satisfied, happy and fulfilled, and when they are balanced within themselves their joy and enthusiasm for life infects everyone around them.

They remind us of the pure pleasure of existence, which is the greatest gift of all. Gluttony is here understood as a passion for pleasure where hedonism invades the psyche (creating confusion) and distances the individual from self-realization. The greedy faces the world with the strategy of words and good reasons, manipulates using the intellect ... as Paolo Quattrini says, his currency is "consensus". He is also a dreamer in the sense that with his quackery he presents dreams as if they were reality, so his "planning" is different from that of 1s and 3s because he also has an expressive and persuasive capacity, he is a manipulator of words, implies that he knows much more than he actually knows. He is cunning, he is the fox of La Fontaine.

His greed is also intense in the sense of wanting "more" in particular in the sense of what is inaccessible and bizarre, the search for variety, adventure and surprise. He is open-minded and dedicated to exploration, seeking new experiences from an unsatisfactory here to an elsewhere full of promise. It does not cling to existing cultural models, but could shift to a utopian, futuristic or innovative vision. Behind the enthusiasm it compensates for the discontent, hides the frustration and prevents the discontent from reaching consciousness. Greedy not for common things but for what is rarer and more extraordinary, in fact he is interested in magic or esotericism as a manifestation of a broader interest in what is distant, remote, on the edge of knowledge.

Hedonistic permissiveness: typical is the avoidance of suffering and the tendency to hedonism to which permissiveness and self-indulgence are linked, which gives it the typical "spoiled" aspect in the sense of feeling entitled to receive any gratification.

Permissiveness is also towards others and often turns into complicity with the vices of others. You feel more than ok and the world is a beautiful place to live where there is no evil and good, duties, etc., but you just need to enjoy it.

Rebellious attitude: the rebellious attitude of the 7 manifests itself, in an inhibited society like ours, in an acuteness for the most common prejudices and which is generally expressed with humorous jokes, or in the nonconformist tendency, while intellectual rebellion accompanies to a certain acquiescence in behavior, in fact the 7 are more ideologues than activists of the revolution. He has no sympathy for authority because he learned from an early age that there are no good authorities and, in any case, he has a more diplomatic attitude towards them than an oppositional one. If the 6 have all too well in mind the quality of the relationships they establish with superiors and inferiors, the 7-approach people with an egalitarian attitude, they do not take authority too seriously, but neither do they propose themselves as authority except in a disguised way.

Lack of discipline: gluttony and a rebellious attitude are expressed in the lack of discipline, instability, lack of commitments and in the typical amateur ways. Typical of playboys: the indolent attitude of one who enjoys it. Lack of discipline is linked to not being able to postpone pleasure because this is experienced as a lack of love. Imaginary fulfillment of wishes: like a baby at the breast, the 7 clings to a world of sweetness and absence of frustration. Here, as an escape from the harsh reality of life, we find the attraction for the future and identification with projects and ideals that seem to live more in fantasy than in concrete reality. A nice seducer: the character is happy, lovable and likeable. Like the 2 he is very seductive and aims to be nice by making himself useful and maintaining a carefree and cheerful attitude.

Generosity is part of seductiveness; it is a way of buying love that compensates for the psychic opposite of the habit of exploitation (tendency to parasitism and perhaps with the feeling of having the right to be cared for and loved).

Sympathy and charm not only serve to seduce but to manipulate and enchant others. So, he has the gift of a hypnotic charm. The satisfied state of the 7 rests on the typical priorities of one who enjoys it, and partly on the ability of the greedy to create an imaginary satisfaction. Feeling good is functional to seductiveness. His good humor infects others.

The happiness of the 7 lives at the expense of the removal and avoidance of pain and results in an impoverishment of the experience. In particular, his coldness is a consequence of the removal of anxiety and chronically feeds his habit of taking refuge in pleasure.

Narcissism: exhibitionist, he knows better than anyone else, well informed, intellectually superior. Characteristics that often manifest themselves as a compulsion to explain things. Seduction through superiority not only intellectual, but can be connoted by religiosity, goodness or holiness with apparent absence of ostentation. They tend to create egalitarian rather than authoritarian fraternal relationships, so the claimed superiority is implicit and disguised behind a modest, warm and equal manner.

The "oral-receptive" personality; the relationship to satisfied narcissism translates into the psychological characteristic of charm: great ability, perceptiveness, savoir vivre and so on and its qualities of sympathy, non-aggression, flexibility, coldness and satisfaction. Convincing: the search for love has become the search for pleasure, satisfying one's desires by bringing out a whole slew of explanations and rationalizations, like the charlatan who manages to convince others of the usefulness of what he sells.

The ability to persuade arises from personal confidence in one's own wisdom, superiority, respectability and goodness of purpose which often takes the form of giving advice and the pleasure of having influence on others, the pleasure of manipulating through words, given his great intelligence, verbal ability and the ability to make suggestions. Fraudulence or charlatanism: in the sense of confusion between reality and fantasy, projects and achievements, potentials and obligations. Sympathy hides anxiety, sweetness hides aggression, generosity hides his approximate behavior for this reason the definition of charlatan suits him.

Kernberg and Kouhut, who identify the psychodynamic etiology of narcissistic psychopathology in the formation of self-esteem: a mother lacking empathy causes the process of idealization to develop in a disturbed way, the subject stops at the level of the archaic infantile grandiose self and research ceaselessly the idealized self-object. The environmental influences can be identified in a prolonged and happy breastfeeding that will lead him to be a confident, optimistic person who has never stopped idealizing his mother and who in the face of life's difficulties returns to his lost paradise.

Common in the history of the seven characters is to rebel quietly against an authoritarian parent or to have a particular bond with the parent of the opposite sex. Crucial for the formation of their character is having a parent of the same character in the family. For these enneatypes, being loved is equal to the fulfillment of their desires, so all their efforts are aimed at the search for pleasure that end up replacing love same. Like the envious, the gluttonous also feels a void inside and tries to fill it with something that comes from outside, but compared to four, seven masks the void with false abundance (as happens in character two). Insufficiency and hedonism create a vicious circle where pleasure takes the place of love, the deepest meanings are lost to obtain immediate benefits.

Furthermore, the subject has to deal with the fear that does not allow him to live a real life. To get away from the frustrations of the present, they take refuge in the search for the arcane, for spirituality, for the paranormal, further fueling the ontic insufficiency.

Defense Mechanisms

The seven character uses different defense mechanisms: idealization, rationalization, hypomania, sublimation, regression. Rationalization serves seven to cover the true motivations of their actions, resorting to arguments, valid reasons to justify its indulging on desires and impulses, in doing so satisfies the superego. Rationalization is the basis of the idealization of the Self (from which narcissism derives), of the mother, of the world and of the people significant to him. Sublimation, on the other hand, induces him to transform his instincts into socially useful things, it also does not allow him to understand that his actions are dictated by his needs and not as he believes by his altruism. Sublimation therefore also explains the fact that this character lives in the imagination by substituting projects, images, for their real objective.

The regression mechanism is used to avoid the present frustrations and take refuge in childhood up to the maternal womb, through hypomania instead, they replace the sadness and pain of the present moment with pleasure and happiness.

Subtypes Conservative subtype

The conservative subtype appears to be the most affectionate of the three, but it is the most cynical, opportunistic, self-indulgent, uses rationalization to get what it wants and projects a good self-image for his own purposes. He idealizes the mother who represents the highest values and is a womanizer who seeks feminine love, maternal love in women. Among the three subtypes, it is the one most linked to the family and with a little more sense of duty

Social subtype

The social subtype is dreamy, imaginative, disguises his selfishness with warmth, idealizes others, especially the father figure.

Sexual subtype

The sexual subtype idealizes itself, in his inner child and promotes himself to obtain external confirmations, gratifications relating to his talents and qualities. He is the most narcissistic, he loves to entertain by talking about himself, preening himself as a person who knows how to feel good in the world, above average, interesting and cultured.

Chapter 9

The Leader or Challenger Enneatype 8

The Challenger because, of all kinds, he is the one who most loves to accept challenges and equally give others opportunities that challenge themselves to overcome themselves. The 8 types are charismatic and possess the physical and psychological characteristics to persuade others to follow them in any business: from starting a business to rebuilding a city, running a house to supporting a war or agreeing on a peace. Type 8s have tremendous willpower and vitality and feel especially alive when exercising these abilities in the world. They use their abundant energy to make changes in their environment, to "leave their mark", but also to protect themselves and their loved ones from being harmed.

From childhood, Eights understand that this requires strength, willpower, perseverance and endurance, qualities that they develop in themselves and seek in others. Type 8s don't want to be controlled and don't allow others to have power over them (their Basic Fear), whether it's psychological, sexual, social or financial power.

They constantly try to increase whatever power they have and to keep it for as long as possible. A type 8 could be a general or a gardener, a small business owner or a tycoon, a mother of a family or a religious leader: the important thing is to be in charge of something and leave your mark. The Eights are the real "avid individualists" of the Enneagram. More than any other type, they function autonomously. They want to be independent and make sure they don't owe anyone.

Often, they refuse to "submit" to social conventions and come to challenge fear, shame and worry about the consequences of their actions. Although they are generally aware of what others think of them, they do not allow themselves to be sidetracked by the opinions of others. They pursue their goals with steely determination, which for others can inspire admiration as well as be intimidating. Although some Eights fear being physically harmed, what scares them most is that their power is being taken away or being controlled in some way. Eights are extraordinarily tough and can endure considerable physical punishment without complaining, which is a double-edged sword as they often take their health and energy for granted, even underestimating those of people close to them.

However, they also have a desperate fear of being emotionally hurt and use physical strength to protect their feelings and keep others at a safe emotional distance. Under a facade of toughness and covered in multi-layered emotional armor lies their vulnerability. So, Eights are often extremely hardworking, but at the cost of losing emotional contact with many of the people in their lives. Those closest to them can thus become increasingly dissatisfied with this state of affairs, displacing them ("I don't understand what my family is complaining about. I go out of my way for them. Why are they not satisfied with me?"). When this happens, Eights feel misunderstood and usually distance themselves even further.

Under their imposing exterior, Eights often feel hurt and rejected, although they rarely talk about it because they struggle to admit their vulnerability with themselves, let alone with others. Because they fear being rejected (left by their spouse, humiliated, criticized, fired or harmed in some way), they try to defend themselves by rejecting others first. The result is that Medium Eight types remain stuck in their inability to get in touch with people, or to love, as love gives others power over them by awakening their Fundamental Fear. The more Eight types strengthen their egos to protect themselves, the more sensitive they become to any slightest affront, real or imagined, to their self-esteem, authority or prominence. The more they try to make themselves insensitive to pain (both physical and emotional), the more they emotionally close and harden like rocks.

Probable history:

As a child, being very noisy and restless, he may have suffered rejection or punishment, so when he grows up he will soon leave home and may become a rebel, the cause is therefore to be found in a family environment lacking care and love but with frequent violence that prompted this character to immediately renounce seeking affection. The proof of love that he requires of others is to let himself be used, possessed, dominated by him. Character eight, being projected on the fight to overwhelm the enemy, loses sight of humanity, delicacy, tenderness and seeks substitutes for being such as pleasure, triumph ... He becomes unable to receive because he wants to dominate, but the knowledge of being takes place by becoming more open and receptive.

Key Character Traits:

Lust

The passion of lust is heralded by the character eight who wants to show the world that it is not bad, it is very evident in him and takes the form of: hedonism, impatience, impulsiveness, excessive desire for excitement, boredom without adequate stimuli. Lust includes not only pleasure but also the struggle for pleasure and a combination of pain and pleasure (the pain it caused in others, the pain to get pleasure) and turns into a passion for intensity, for struggle which includes triumph.

Punitive attitude. The character eight can also be defined as sadistic, hostile, who wants to humiliate. His fixation is revenge, which is not open and driven by hatred as in character four but is long-term, the eight becomes an executioner: he takes revenge to overturn the situation of pain and humiliation suffered as a child. Sadism is given by the transformation of one's frustrations and humiliations, by the excitement caused by intense stimuli, in short, the pain suffered made him numb. The punitive attitude is the fixation of character eight, it serves to take revenge and is the result of his anger.

Rebellious attitude. He becomes rebellious and evil, opposes authority (especially his father, considered an illegitimate power), despises the values of morality and education.

Arrogance. It is a characteristic related to hostility and is useful for revenge along with devaluation and contempt for others.

Insensitivity This character has become hardened, embittered, it has driven away fear, sentimentality, pity; for him the anxiety generated by risk is not suffering but, due to an indirect masochistic mechanism, it has turned into pleasure, in the salt of his life.

Despotism and cynicism. These two linked traits coincide in Fromm's (1971) description of skepticism.

Exhibitionism (Narcissism). This character also has a funny, seductive, witty aspect that he uses for manipulative purposes, to gain power and to be liked by others.

Autonomy. The eight idealizes autonomy, rejects dependence and passive oral desires.

Sensorimotor predominance

Prevalence of action over thought and feeling. He lives and focuses on the present because he considers unreal everything that he cannot verify with his senses.

Defense mechanisms. These subjects do not seem to use defenses because they appear freer than others, they indulge in anger, they live sexuality intensely, they do not inhibit their impulses, Reich, in the phallic - narcissistic character, explains this characteristic as a defense against dependence and passivity. In fact, they defend themselves by repressing their need for love, tenderness, in doing so they harden.

The defense mechanisms most used by this character are denial and desensitization; one works more on a cognitive level by suppressing the feelings of guilt given by his contemptuous attitude towards others and represses intuition (disinterest in the psychology of others), the other acts more on a sensory and affective level and has to do with the nullification of physical, emotional pain and fear. On a psychological level, it happens that risky situations turn into excitement, challenge, through an act of sadism towards oneself, in practice the subject has given up loving himself and receiving love from others.

Desensitization induces this character to invert traditional values so that the atrocities he does always have a purpose of justice and he always appears on the side of the 'good', this mechanism could be described as counter-identification, (his rebellious nature contributes), in practice it is an inverse identification with what parents and society preach. Compared to character four which interjects bad objects as foreign bodies, character eight through counter-identifications puts out of itself what it does not want.

Sub types

Conservative subtype. In the conservative subtype, desensitization is more evident, it is the hardest, the least emotional of the three subtypes, it is the most selfish and the most aggressive because all its energy is used for survival at all costs, skilled in bargaining for the purpose to get the maximum benefits. An image that represents this subject well is the solitary knight, closed in on himself, taciturn.

Social Subtype. The social subtype is a little more compassionate than the conservative, slightly more sensitive, especially when it witnesses an injustice it becomes empathetic and supportive. He is more sociable, more open to others, but he remains the undisputed authority.

Sexual subtype. The sexual subtype is, among the three, the most emotional, even if of course it does not feel physical pain, it is able to withstand fatigue, hard jobs, diseases, wars. He lives in a state of constant challenge, putting his life in serious danger with brazenness and optimism. An image that represents him can be that of a mercenary soldier.

Academic psychological parallels. Naranjo finds in the eight the description of Schneider's 'explosive' personality characterized by distrust, disobedience, outbursts of anger at the slightest provocation. Sholtz speaks of "moral anesthesia" about this kind of contemptuous character of morality. For Naranjo, character eight corresponds to Kraeplin's psychopathic personality and Millon's sociopaths, Cleckey describes their main traits: lack of guilt, impulsiveness, emotional emptiness, inability to object love.

Reich, in Character Analysis speaks of a 'narcissistic phallic personality', characterized by an arrogant or distant, reserved or aggressive behavior, with a narcissistic element that is expressed through libidinous and sadistic aspects towards the object of love

and in displaying a great self-confidence, moreover aggression is channeled into attacking to prevent any attacks. Fromm describes 'appropriative orientation': hostile and manipulative subjects who steal things from others with strength and cunning, not expecting to receive them as a gift.

Horney, in a work read in 1948 at the Association for the Advancement of Psychoanalysis and then published in the American Journal of Psychoanalisis, replaces the term 'sadistic' with 'openly aggressive vengefulness' and speaks of a vindictive character very similar to the eight: the subject identifies with his grandiose self, has a desire for dominoes to hide weakness and incapacity, has a powerful impulse and weak inhibitions, he is convinced that the world is malevolent and perverse so he behaves in a rude and offensive way, humiliates and exploits others to achieve his ends, he does not care about the needs and desires of others, being isolated and hostile he tries to never need others.

This attitude of his leads him to exclude joy, happiness, love from his life. His arrogance doesn't make him admit that he actually envies others because he thinks they are better than him. In Jung, the 'extroverted sensorial' type corresponds to the eight regarding the aspects of lust, realism, the search for intense sensations, but it is not present in the aspect of dominance.

Chapter 10:

The Diplomat or Peacemaker Enneatype 9

Nine types are welcoming, confident, and balanced. They are usually creative, optimistic, and supportive, but may tend to be too compliant to keep the peace. They want everything to go smoothly and be conflict-free, but they tend to feel smug, simplifying problems and minimizing whatever is bothering. They typically have problems with indolence and stubbornness. Psychological inertia: inner poverty is to be understood as a lack of fire, a phlegm from which any passion is absent, which on an intellectual level is visible in dullness and lack of imagination. Not wanting to see, not wanting to be in contact with one's own experience resembles the laziness of those who do not want to know, an eclipse of knowledge consistent with the disposition to concreteness, with a materialistic attitude to the bitter end, a practical sense at the expense of understanding and mystery.

We have called the Nine The Peacemaker, because no other type desires more inner and outer peace for themselves and others. They are the typical "spiritual seekers" who have an enormous longing to connect with the cosmos as well as with other people. They work to maintain their own peace of mind, as well as to establish peace and harmony in their world. The themes encountered in the Nine are fundamental for any spiritual or psychological path: awakening as opposed to falling asleep to one's nature, presence as opposed to trance, tension opposed to relaxation, peace opposed to suffering, union opposed to separation.

Ironically for a guy so inclined to the spiritual world, he is in the nuclear point of the Instinct Center and is potentially the most rooted type in the physical world and in his own body.

The contradiction is explained when we realize that Nine types are either in touch with their instinctive qualities and have enormous natural power and personal magnetism, or they are alienated from their own instinctive strength and can be disengaged, absent and even etheric. Being out of touch with their own instinctive energies, the Nine withdraw into their minds and emotional fantasies (This is why Nine types can mistakenly identify with Fives or Seven who are "head types", or with Type Twos or Fours who are "emotional types.") Also, when their instinctive energies are out of balance, type Nine use them against themselves, holding onto their potency, until everything in their psyche becomes static and helpless. When this energy is not used, it stagnates like a pond into which all the water of a stream pours and becomes so full that it blocks the same stream that feeds it. However, when Nine types are in balance with their Instinctive Center and their energy, they are like a great river carrying everything effortlessly.

We have sometimes called the Nine the crown of the Enneagram because it is at the highest point of the symbol and seems to include it entirely. Nines may have the strength of the Eight, the sense of fun and adventure of the Seven, the sense of duty of the Six, the intellectualism of the Five, the creativity of the Four, the charm of the Three, the generosity of the Two and the idealism of the One.

However, what they generally do not have is the feeling of actually inhabiting themselves: a strong sense of their own identity. So ironically the only type the Nine doesn't look like is your own. It is terrifying for the Nine to be a separate individual who has to assert himself against others; he prefers to merge with someone else or quietly follow his own idyllic daydreams.

The Nine types are the living demonstration of the common temptation to all to ignore the disturbing aspects of life seeking peace and comfort in numbness. They react to pain and suffering by attempting to live in a premature state of peace, in a condition of false spiritual realization, or in obvious denial. More than any other type, the Nine show a tendency to escape the paradoxes and tensions of life, attempting to transcend them or seeking simple and painless solutions to their problems.

Emphasizing what is pleasant in life is obviously not a bad thing in itself, but it is a somewhat limited and limiting approach. Just as Nine types see the silver lining in any ailment as a way to protect themselves from the elements of life, other types have their own distorted views. For example, the Four focus on their own wounds and victimhood, the Ones focus on what is wrong, and so on. By contrast, Nines tend to focus on the good side of life so that their peace is not shaken. But rather than denying the negative side of life, what the Nines need to understand is that all perspectives of the other types are equally true. Type Nine must resist the urge to withdraw into a premature state of Nirvana, or into the "divine light" away from the earthly world. They must remember that "the only way out is across".

Hyperadaptation: if passion is spiritual laziness, interpersonal strategy and the concept of life can be defined with expressions such as "hyperadaptation", "self-denial", "neglect of personal needs" and "inclination to excessive control", what not possible without, in fact, the ability to hold back and inhibit one's impulses. In fact, we often find in 9 a propensity for alcohol or food as compensations. Expressions such as determined, responsible, dependent and generous in the sense that 9s always end up "pulling the cart" and are always ready to load themselves with weights.

Resignation: in 9s the inability to love others as oneself is overturned: it puts one's needs in the background with great surrender and this implies resignation. His survival strategy seems to be "playing dead", only in this way he fatally becomes a living dead in the name of life.

Generosity: the 9s, having a dominant propensity to acquiescence, are jovial, generous, outgoing and friendly, they take themselves lightly so as not to weigh on others.

Shapelessness: they are modest types, absolutely not worried about excelling or shining, often ending up also neglecting their physical appearance, always in light of the fact that they have given up a leading position. For them, value consists not so much in applause, as in substitutive participation in living through others. Renunciation of the self is replaced by symbiosis with family identity, nation, party, club, etc.

Automaton habits: they are linked to methodology and regularity and are very concerned about safeguarding their balance, which is why they tend to be conservative and attached to tradition to the point of becoming rigid. In fact, psychological inertia makes them very attached to the rules of the family, of the group or of "the way of doing things". This automatism is the consequence of the renunciation of the self, and this diligence and patience which is rooted in psychological comfort is very striking.

Easy to get distracted: the strategy of 9 is to not see, to narcotize oneself, things that translate into an extreme simplification of the external and internal world. Often, he describes himself as a distracted and confused person, sometimes with poor memory, as a sign of attention that moves to the periphery rather than to the center of the world of experience.

Defense mechanisms

The following mechanisms are present: deflection, confluence, hypomanic joviality. The deflection (in this case it can simply be called distraction) is a mechanism of the interruption of contact that the subject nine adopts towards himself and towards

others, for example by diverting, diverting attention from intense emotions, not answering questions, speaking in the abstract. So he wanders, gets lost in unimportant things or throws himself into action moved by a simplistic and concrete vision of life. Nine can use hypomanic joviality as a defense to avoid negative emotions and to hide depression. Confluence causes the subject to identify with the others; ideas and needs of others become his adapting easily to the other, just as happens in the symbiotic mother-child relationship.

The conservative subtype anesthetizes itself much more than the other subtypes. The social is more active but its purpose is always to keep peace, the sexual puts its energy into sexuality, but compared to the sexual eight it is more monogamous and calmer, in general the three subtypes have a softer physicality, they are similar to the eight but more muffled.

Academic psychological parallels: Naranjo cites Kretschmer because in the cyclothymic syndrome in Anatomy and Character he revises type nine and reports its most frequent characteristics:

1- Sociable, kind-hearted, friendly, brilliant 2- Cheerful, witty, lively, hasty

3- Quiet, calm, easily depressed, easily moved

Sheldon, in The Varieties of Temperament, describes the viscerotonia that fits a lot with the nine: "Viscerotonia manifests itself with relaxation, conviviality, gluttony, the need for company, affection or social support. When this component is predominant, the primary motivation of life seems to be adaptation and energy saving ". Arieti, in Affective Disorders, names two types of depression: the vindictive one, which Naranjo finds most in character four, and the self-reproving one, which suits character nine more. In the transitional

analysis, Naranjo mentions the figure of a mother who gives up to wear out because she devalues, in Jung, we find the nine in the introverted feeling type, especially very common in women.

Chapter 11

Subtypes

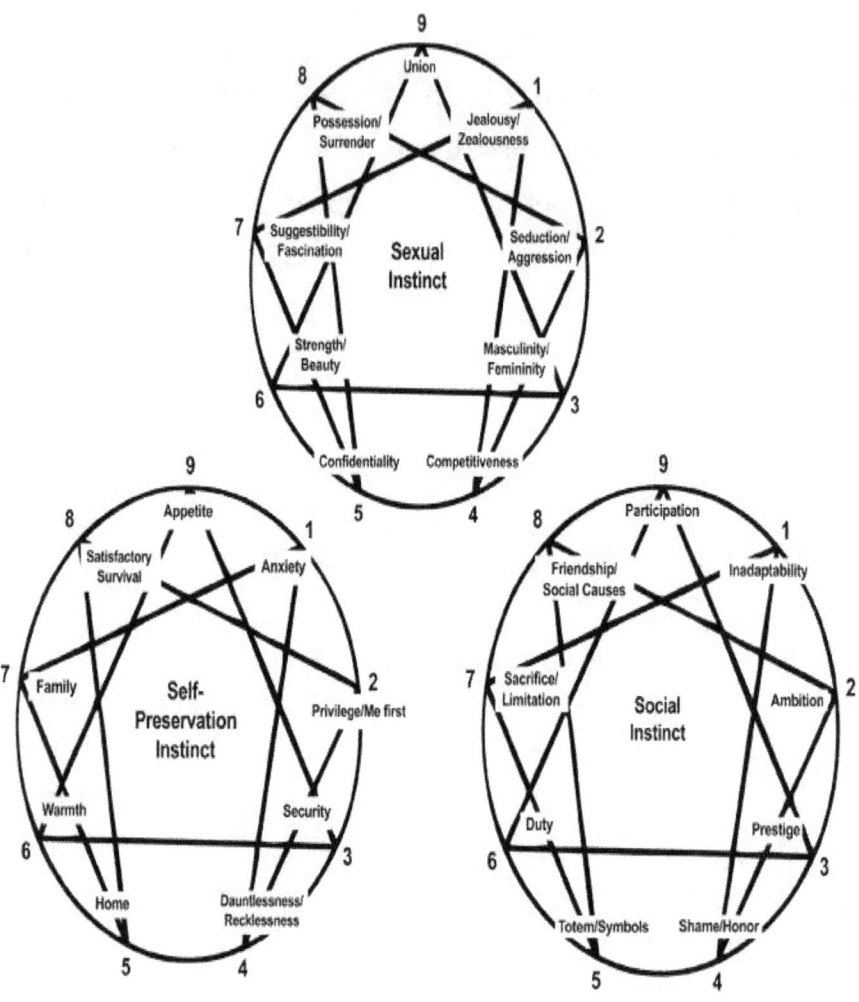

As we have seen, a further subdivision of the enneagram is that of the so-called subtypes.

That is, each character is in turn divided into 3 subtypes:

instinctual (expansive tendency), rational (retractive tendency) emotional (adaptive tendency).

We can therefore propose a further specification of the three intelligences and therefore of the subtypes:

those who prefer to acquire energy, in the sense of having it to use, TEND TO

EXPANDING, therefore have an EXPANSIVE attitude which is the basic one of instinctual 8 - 9 - 1;

those who tend to avoid energy losses as much as possible, TEND TO RETRACT, therefore have a RETRACTIVE attitude which is the basic one of rational 5-6-7;

those who tend to use energy in the surrounding environment, TEND TO ADAPT, that is, have an ADAPTIVE or RELATIONAL attitude, with the environment and others, which is typical of the 2-3-4 emotional base.

Finally, there are three characterizing thematic variants that enter into relation with the fundamental themes of one's intelligence which are:

ANGER;

FEAR;

SHAME.

Then we can further specify the characters and the three intelligences as follows:

Instinctual (Expansive / Sexual) 8, 9, 1 with a characterizing theme of ANGER;

Emotional (Adaptive / Social) 2, 3, 4 with a characterizing theme SHAME;

Rationals (Retractives / Conservatives) 5, 6, 7 with a theme characterizing FEAR; which reverberated in the SUB-TYPES correspond to:

that of EXPANSION determined by ANGER;

that of ADAPTATION determined by SHAME;

that of RETRACTION determined by FEAR.

Finally, there are three aspects or levels of behavior for each subtype:

integrated;

medium-low;

disrupted.

The description of the subtypes that is usually explained refers to the medium-low level, that is the one with which one normally encounters in everyday life. Without going into each subtype, we can give some brief indications.

While it is not possible for the characters to make the quantum jump (that is, to switch from one character to another), it is instead possible to change the subtype: it happens in conjunction with important events in one's life (shock). In the normality of daily life this does not happen because without a crisis on the horizon there is no need to access new resources.

The rational subtype (retraction) favors the relationship with oneself; The emotional subtype (adaptation) favors the relationship with the group; The instinctual (expansion) subtype favors the relationship of two.

The emotional (social) subtype in the relationship with the world and with others raises the following three questions:

8 9 1 = "How can I show how I am in the environment?";

2 3 4 = "How do I relate to the environment?";

5 6 7 = "How can I accept the requests of the world?".

The focus is on the need to be part of a group or community. It usually focuses on a desire or concern to be with someone more important than oneself, to be recognized, accepted, approved and loved. You want status and well-being. It is an impulse to belong, to be part of.

The rational (conservative) subtype in the relationship with the world and with others arises

the following three questions:

8 9 1 = "How can I survive in the environment?";

2 3 4 = "How can I protect myself from the environment?";

5 6 7 = "How can I hide from the demands of the world?".

The need to be satisfied is that of safety and physical and emotional comfort. Usually this means that there is a form of concern about food, about having a place to shelter, about having physical and mental, economic and health security. Look for a sense of well- being and self-protection. It has an impulse to feel secure.

The instinctual (sexual) subtype in the relationship with the world and with others raises the following three questions:

8 9 1 = "How can I own the environment?

2 3 4 = "How can I win over others?"

5 6 7 = "How can I meet the demands of the world?"

The focus is on the need for intimacy and the sense of connection and special relationship with another. There is a concern about relationships to believe in and build upon. A search for an intense personal experience and a drive for union.

Continuing in the wake of character 2 as an example, a brief description of its three subtypes could be this:

Character 2, subtype Instinctual (expansive I sexual).

Pride + expansion = aggression / seduction. Shame + Anger.

Key word SEDUCTIVITY.

He conquers everyone, goes towards the other, never takes a back seat.

It is the type 2 most like a 2 than all others.

The freest, the wildest. Sensuality / sexuality that liberates without problems. With its freedom, it can also be confused with an 8 character.

He puts all his charm to work to trap the other. Try to create and to be addicted to the other, because the desire of the other provides him with nourishment. It is the subtype that is easily found in a triangular relationship. It is very direct.

Example: Casanova. Character 2, subtype Emotional (adaptive / social) pride + adaptation = ambition.

Shame + Shame. Keyword AMBITION.

He sits on the right hand of the Father.

They don't want success as much as they want to play a significant role alongside socially significant people. Compelling, histrionic, brilliant, lover of knowledge. A little colder than the other two subtypes. It is a mix of seductiveness, manipulation, cognitiveability. His idea is: "I want everyone to realize how special I am." He feels he has to do something in the service of someone, for the good of the nation, of humanity, something great, however high. Example:

Napoleon.

Character 2, subtype Rational (retractive / conservative). pride + retraction = caprice (privilege).

Shame + Fear. Keyword CAPRICE.

Less needy than the "public", He wants to have from others.

He is the child at the center of the world.

Very sensual, a lot of tenderness in the relationship.

Tenderness, whim and seductive conquest.

Privilege and merit to enjoy particular privileges thanks to his goodness and his human availability. He asks proudly. It gives itself value. It is strongly demanding. He does not share his things as he is afraid of running out.

His specific question is: "What can I do to please you?" It is the so-called counter-2. Examples: Liz Taylor and P. Pravo.

We have said that in order to identify one's typology, one must learn to become observers of oneself. Which is not introspection but observation of how we act (instinctive center), how we feel (emotional center) and how we think (mental center) to recognize the automatic reactions of the personality.

In this way, having identified our type, we will be able to move towards the recovery of the ability to react to life in a non-automatic but objective way and in harmony with the true ego, bringing to light hidden and unused potentials. This will give us the awareness that we have a wide opportunity to understand our being in the world and to correct with great freedom what is not functional for us. It is not a question of transcending or subduing the personality but of assisting it and understanding the direction it indicates to us. It is like removing what is not needed to let the shape that is close to the heart emerge.

Self-observation also has the very important function of awakening the awareness of Self, of one's own Inner Master Observer, who gradually perceives himself as different from the observed personality.

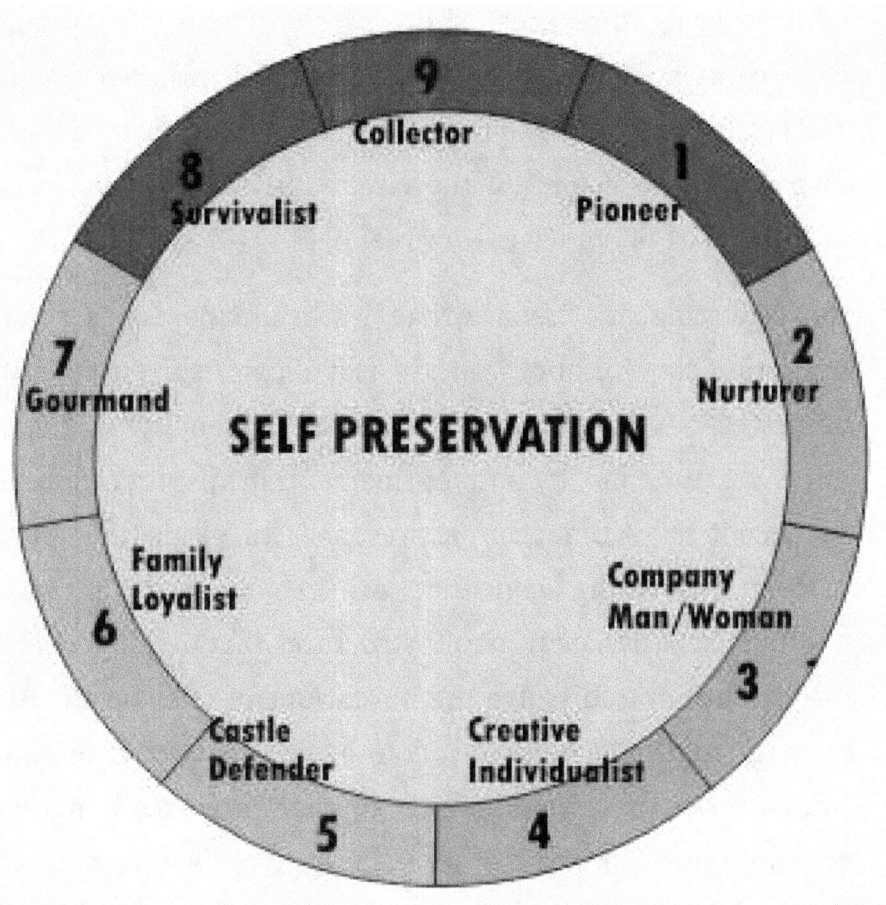

Rediscovering the voice of one's self of one's Immutable Essence means going beyond the limits of one's personality and getting in touch with the spiritual dimension which in the diagram is the center of the circle and which is the most intimate part of ourselves, our real part.

Rediscovering the Essence that lies in our depths is a very important step for our evolution as it allows us to emancipate ourselves from the conditioning of the personality and open ourselves to a more complete perception of ourselves, the Essence itself, with its simple presence, will guide the path, It is the transforming agent that with its strength gives us the ability to separate us from old structures that no longer serve our evolution, to dissolve the limitations of false personality from the mind The meaning of our evolution is not to dissolve into a more or less indefinite all that provokes a natural resistance for fear of dissolution, but is to rediscover the well-being of the child whose memory remains in us.

Chapter 12

How to Recognize Your Type

Identifying the psychological type to which one belongs will lead us towards a deeper knowledge of our personal identity, which does not mean becoming other than oneself but recognizing the mask we wear and in which we are identified. To begin to overcome it, freeing ourselves from the limits of repetitive behaviors by attenuating the aspects that involve more discomfort and giving space to the positive aspects of all kinds, in fact each type can be defined as a psychological family that has in common a set of particular automatisms that regulate attitudes and behaviors that, once recognized, become aware of them, can be managed, diluted and exploited in our favor.

This inevitably leads to a personal growth that advances from the current situation, whatever it is, to the level we want to reach, to lead a daily life in which our behavioral choices are aware and not deriving from unconscious automatisms, which re-propose, for every situation, the same solution.

Knowing and understanding the different types of personalities, finding oneself in one in particular and starting to recognize the people around us should lead to a truer relationship life, perceiving ourselves and others no longer through projections and personal beliefs but through the image we have of ourselves.

This will allow us to face events with a different attitude. Studying the various types and then proceeding to observe carefully and accurately our reactions to find your type is an opportunity for personal awareness that must lead us to strengthen self-knowledge, without considering it a definitive or limiting classification, but using it to progress in our personal growth, understanding that the personality is the key element of the individual spiritual path.

The nine personality types described by the Enneagram, are all endowed with positive and negative traits, and, although each type has well- defined characteristics in which it is possible to recognize itself, nevertheless the real experience, that is, how these main characteristics are expressed in everyday life, are absolutely peculiar to each and make it a unique being.

The important thing is to honestly identify our personality, only our true fundamental type will lead us to a path of awareness, indeed, it is advisable not to discard a type a priori because it does not correspond to our ideal of person because this could mean that there are of the blocks towards the real knowledge of ourselves. We will thus be able to avoid developing possibilities of another type in which we want to recognize ourselves because perhaps we like it more, but it would be a false path that would lead us nowhere.

Often what we do not accept about ourselves are unresolved aspects that cause us inner and energetic blocks, the aspects that we do not accept are, at times, the main lessons we must learn. One difficulty in recognizing ourselves as a type is given by the defense mechanisms that prevent us from seeing our negative traits, so we need that much detachment that allows us to observe the most objective possible.

Personal growth is like embarking on a journey and it is useful to identify the exact point where you are and what obstacles you may encounter, with the Enneagram it is possible, by identifying the main characteristic, to know in which point of the circumference we are and that is which personality we are.

The personality also shapes the physical aspect so identifying the physical characteristics can help to identify an enneatype, a hint of these characteristics will be given by treating the various types.

www.ingramcontent.com/pod-product-compliance
Lightning Source LLC
Chambersburg PA
CBHW071453080526
44587CB00014B/2096